OWNING WESTERN HISTORY

OWNING WESTERN HISTORY

A Guide to Collecting Rare Documents, Historical
Letters, and Valuable Autographs from the Old West

Warren R. Anderson

Mountain Press Publishing Company
Missoula, Montana
1993

Copyright © 1993
Warren R. Anderson

Library of Congress Cataloging-in-Publication Data

Anderson, Warren R., 1953-
  Owning western history : a guide to collecting rare documents, historical letters, and valuable autographs from the Old West / Warren R. Anderson.
      p.   cm.
  Includes bibliographical references and index.
  ISNB 0-87842-285-4 : $15.00
  1. Manuscripts, American—Collectors and collecting—United States.   2. Legal documents—Collectors and collecting—United States.   3. Americana—Collectors and collecting—United States. 4. Americana—West (U.S.)   I. Title.
Z987.5.U6A46   1993
978 ' .02 ' 075—dc20   92-45718
                                                                         CIP

MOUNTAIN PRESS PUBLISHING COMPANY
P.O. Box 2399 • Missoula, MT 59806
(406) 728-1900 • (800) 234-5308

Contents

Foreword vi

Acknowledgements vii

About the Author vii

Introduction 1

Chapters

    1. Paper Americana 3

    2. Evaluating Documents 14

    3. Autographs 25

    4. Content 35

    5. Fakes, Forgeries, and Thefts 43

    6. Assessing Documents, Conditions, Cancellations,
       and Revenue Stamps 57

    7. Establishing Your Collection 69

    8. Nearly Everything You Want to Know
       About Auctions and Dealers 86

Appendices

    A. Types of Collectible Documents 91

    B. Statehood Dates and Boundaries 108

    C. Collecting and Historical Organizations 111

Glossary 113

Bibliography 115

Index 117

Foreword

In composing *Owning Western History*, author Warren Anderson breaks with the traditional practice of writing about western history by telling his readers how to *collect* western history, specifically important and rare documents, letters, and autographs. This book explores the world of historical document dealings and offers a unique and fascinating look into the fastest growing collecting field in western americana.

This collector's guide is a ground-breaking effort destined to become a standard reference work for both private and public collectors as well as western history buffs, archivists, librarians, museums, appraisers, historians, rare book dealers, and others who come into contact with old documents. It fills a long-standing void of information that has hampered our understanding and workings of the marketplace. This important and timely information will prove beneficial to the readers.

The author is well known for his research and writings about historical western documents, and in this book he examines a broad range of topics from auctions and forgeries to collecting boundaries and document content. The numerous personal experiences he shares with readers come from his many years of knowledge as both a dealer and collector, working with both institutional and private clients.

Owning Western History is highlighted by scores of photographs of western documents ranging from inexpensive items to the rarest of documents, including previously unpublished photographs of documents signed by such famous westerners as Butch Cassidy, Wyatt Earp, Jesse James, and many other famous Westerners.

In recent years Warren Anderson has emerged as one of the leading figures in the collection, preservation and study of documents relating to the American West. These documents are not merely curiosities or museum pieces to him. While they often have significant visual appeal in an aesthetic sense, the documents he collects, studies and interprets offer important windows into the nature of Western history.

Gary Topping
Former Curator of Manuscripts
Utah State Historical Society

Acknowledgements

Many people have inspired me in various ways since I began my journey into historical document collecting in 1979, and I owe them my thanks. My parents, Jerry and Daisy Anderson, nurtured my interest in western history with books, vacations, museum visits, and annual camping trips to our family's mining claims in the Mojave Desert. My adventuresome brothers, Tim and Perry, have helped keep this interest alive through our summer camping excursions to ghost towns and mining districts.

Charles Kemp, Gene Hessler, and William Weiss, Jr., provided valuable assistance, as did Frain Pearson, George Throckmorton, Gary Topping, Con Psarras, Ron Englestead, Sharon and Bob Huxford, and Barry Church. And I must thank Dr. Robert Anthony, who taught me that there are two things in life—reasons and results—and reasons don't count.

Some of the documents illustrated came from Craig Fouts' collection. I appreciate his assistance in sharing some of his rare discoveries. My thanks to Al Rust, who provided the Mark Hofmann forgery photographs, and Boyd Redington, who photographed many of the documents used in this book.

I wish I could personally thank two good ol' boys who helped me learn the ropes and are now collecting heavenly manuscripts: Jerry Rillahan, a founder of American scripophily, and Walt Alcott, a paper Americana dealer. Many other collectors and dealers I have met over the years have provided input in one form or another, and I thank them for their friendship and knowledge.

About the Author

Warren Anderson has been active in the field of western paper Americana as a collector, dealer, researcher, and writer since 1979.

He serves as an advisor for the annual Schroeder's Antiques Price Guide and is an editorial advisor for Autograph Collector's Magazine. In addition, Anderson is an active member in numerous collecting and historical organizations, including the World Association of Document Examiners. He has written extensively on paper Americana and western history, and some of his articles have appeared in *True West*, *Personal Finance*, *A.B. Bookman's Weekly*, *The Westerner*, *Lost Treasure*, and *Illinois Banker*.

In the "color country" of Cedar City, Utah, Warren lives with his wife, Cheryl, and their five children, and runs America West Archives, his historical documents business.

Introduction

There is no era in American history that inspires as many books, movies, works of art, television series, and public interest as that period of exploration and colonization in the western half of the United States between 1840 and 1910. Events and relics from this period stir some degree of interest in just about everyone, everywhere.

For many years, even before the era ended, collectors gathered cowboy and Indian memorabilia, mostly ignoring other fields of western Americana. Among today's more popular western collectibles are old bottles, weapons, photographs, prints, mining and railroad equipment, furniture, tokens, farm and ranch implements, paintings, and books. Those who collect such items enjoy discovering and caring for rare, authentic remnants of our western heritage. It gives us an opportunity to *own* a piece of western history.

Add now to that list of collectibles another field of western Americana long overlooked and undervalued—that of rare and historical documents associated with the American West. What kinds of documents, you might ask? Primarily those signed by famous Westerners or those that capture the imagination and spirit of pioneer heritage. Documents with special meaning or important content reveal the past in a way that is sometimes lacking in narrative accounts.

I began collecting historical western documents in 1972 in an extraordinary way. I was on a spring picnic with friends near the foothills of Mount Pleasant, a small town in central Utah. We settled on a spot close to a freshly plowed field that surrounded an old, dilapidated pioneer cabin. My curiousity about the decaying building drove me to explore it. Little did I realize then that I was beginning my journey into the world of collecting historical documents.

The deserted cabin contained a surprising conglomeration of household and personal items scattered about. In one room I saw an old shoe box on the floor. I opened it and found a number of old papers and folded documents. When I removed them I saw that they had concealed several corroded sticks of dynamite in the bottom of the box, so I gently set it down and tiptoed out of the cabin with the papers in hand.

My friend, whose family owned the property, shrugged at the sight of the documents and said they were of no importance and that I could have them. Dates on the legal deeds, insurance policies, receipts, and various personal papers ranged from 1880 to 1910. The most attractive document in the lot was an 1888 land grant for forty acres in "Utah Territory" bearing the signature of President Grover Cleveland (actually a proxy by one of his secretaries). The grant had an orange embossed seal with an illustration of a farmer plowing. What really caught my eye, though, was the elegant penmanship that graced the document. Such formal yet fanciful strokes of the pen is an art form virtually lost in our present culture.

This land grant became the first document in my collection, although I didn't begin collecting seriously until seven years later, in 1979, after a friend and I began discussing collectibles with investment potential. I told him about the old documents I found and finally decided to investigate the field of collecting western paper Americana.

Little information has so far been available to the general public on collecting western historical documents. As a result, the field has long remained the domain of institutions and those few collectors who got started before the collecting boom hit in the 1980s. I hope this book will prove a solid introduction and reliable reference to collecting western paper Americana, thus opening the field to new collectors and enhancing the market for quality collectibles.

To my knowledge this is the first book that explains how to go about collecting historic western documents. The information is based on my experiences—some of which I learned the hard way—while buying, selling, and collecting western paper Americana over the years. The knowledge I share here should apply equally well to collecting historical documents from fields other than the American West. Whether you collect documents from the Civil War, the colonial period, or from your home state, there is something in this book for everyone. Its purpose goes beyond simply explaining the fundamentals of collecting and includes such topics as the importance of autographs, what types of documents are suitable for collecting, how to evaluate a document before buying it, how to establish boundaries for your collection, caring for your collection, and much more. Reading it will help new collectors start on a solid foundation.

Beginning a collection always takes some time and effort, but this book should make charting a course into this fascinating and rewarding field easier. All you need is an interest in western history—that's the common bond among its many collectors.

CHAPTER ONE

Paper Americana

One of the first misconceptions newcomers to the field of collecting western paper Americana must overcome is the assumption that historic documents are available only to curators and archivists in libraries, universities, and museums. While it is true that such institutions buy, store, and sometimes trade historical papers, there are also many individuals who treasure their own private collections of paper trails to the past.

For many decades scholars and archivists in public and private institutions, libraries, and museums dominated the field of collecting historical documents and manuscripts; they served as the guardians of these papers for the sake of preservation. Unfortunately, many of these documents were filed so deeply in repositories that they were rarely displayed or seen, much less studied or enjoyed, by the public for whom they were preserved.

For about two decades now this situation has been changing. Groups of documents and manuscripts are finding their way onto the collectibles market and into the collections of private collectors who have begun to discover that they, too, can purchase and own original and historic papers from our country's past.

Collectors come from all walks of life and include professionals from such diverse fields as education, the military, medicine, real estate, banking and finance, law enforcement, mining, entertainment, and many other areas. Collectors sometimes specialize in an area associated with their profession. Someone in mining, for example, may choose to collect defunct claims, assay reports, stock certificates, and other mining-related documents. A police officer may be interested in wanted posters and arrest warrants or autographs of western sheriffs and criminals. A banker might collect old checks, currency, and other financial documents. Another common interest that brings collectors together is an interest in either western history or paper collectibles.

Can you imagine holding a letter handwritten by John C. Frémont to his wife, Jessie, explaining his involvement in California's Bear Flag Revolt? Or how about reading a letter homesick outlaw Butch Cassidy wrote to his brother? Perhaps you'd rather have a colorful 1860s stock certificate hanging on your wall from the American Express Company signed by Henry Wells and James Fargo, founders of Wells, Fargo & Company; or a formal military comdate

BAIL BOND.   El Paso Steam Printing Co., Printers, and Blank Book Makers.

THE STATE OF TEXAS,
County of El Paso } ss.

Know all Men by these Presents, That we Jno. W. Hardin

....as Principal, and

....

as Sureties, are held and firmly bound to pay unto THE STATE OF TEXAS, in the penal sum of

One hundred ....DOLLARS

for the payment of which sum, well and truly to be made, we do bind ourselves and each of us, our heirs, executors and administrators, jointly and severally, by these presents.

Signed and dated this 13th day of May 1895

THE CONDITION OF THE ABOVE OBLIGATION IS SUCH, That whereas the above named principal stands charged by information duly filed in the County Court of El Paso County, Texas, with the offense of *

Betting at a table and game played with dice

NOW, if the said Jno W Hardin shall well and truly
                                now in session
make his personal appearance before said Court ~~at its next term to be begun and holden~~ at the Court House of said County of El Paso in the City of El Paso on the

Instance

and there remain from day to day and term to term of said Court until discharged by due course of law, then and there to answer said accusation against him, this obligation shall become void. Otherwise to remain in full force and effect.

John W Hardin ....Principal.

Approved on this, the..
day of......................18....   E. J. Syme
                                         E. J. Bridges
Sheriff..............Co., Texas.   } SURETIES.
By..............................Deputy.

* Here state the offense as charged in the Indictment or Information, being careful to state it fully and correctly.

Considered one of the most violent gunfighters in the West, John Wesley Hardin killed over two dozen men during his lifetime. Texas Rangers arrested him in 1878 and he spent sixteen years in prison until being pardoned in 1894. He later became a lawyer and practiced in El Paso. Then gambling and drinking caught up with him as this document charging him with illegal gambling shows. Three months after signing it Hardin was shot and killed by rival gunman John Selman while drinking in a bar.

mission signed by President Grover Cleveland promoting an officer and recognizing him for bravery "in action against the Indians at the Caves, Arizona Territory, December, 1878."

These examples of how you can "own" western history represent a small sampling of what ends up on the collectors' market. One treasure I recently encountered was an I.O.U. signed by the notorious gunman John Wesley Hardin for his gambling losses and drinking expenses in an El Paso bar about a month before his murder. His shaky signature suggests he signed it at the end of the night; perhaps his intoxication contributed to his gambling losses. Such documents sometimes reveal much about western history. This collecting field is where western history and paper Americana merge.

Western paper Americana sometimes draws collectors from other fields. For example, some autograph collectors may also want documents signed by famous Westerners; or philatelists (stamp collectors) may look for early western envelopes (covers) bearing particular postmarks or stamps, showing where the mail was processed or identifying certain regional mail carriers.

Some documents are worth only a few dollars; others may be worth thousands. A beginning collector must learn to evaluate a document's content and importance, estimate its value, and determine whether its market price is fair. You can develop a sense for this by perusing dealers' catalogs, searching for specific items at auctions, and attending collectors' shows to consider the historical importance of those documents you know something about.

You can usually determine a document's collector value by evaluating its content or signatures, but its date or place of origin may also prove important. Even after many years of searching you might never see something like a Tombstone arrest warrant signed by Wyatt Earp for sale. But a plain-looking, handwritten receipt from Fort Lewis, Colorado, bearing an 1879 date could be historically important because the fort was still under construction at that time.

Good collections clearly reflect the boundaries their owners build into them. I have purchased haphazard document collections on many occasions that contained perhaps 20 percent quality material, 30 percent good material, and 50 percent common-grade material. It is important to value the *quality* of your collection over its *quantity*, just as a coin collector might avoid building a collection of rare, uncirculated, low-mintage silver dollars augmented by lots of common-grade pennies.

Collecting rare and important western documents is not for everyone. It's an acquired taste. And you must appreciate western history. But seeing a good collection, whether private or public, can really excite and motivate potential collectors. The joy in collecting and owning western history is probably similar to the feelings of pride, accomplishment, and stewardship experienced by collectors of fine art, coins, stamps, or numerous other investment-grade collectibles.

I can think of at least five good reasons to collect western paper Americana: 1) the field has been largely overlooked; 2) many of the documents are undervalued; 3) it's common to encounter rare, often one-of-a-kind, documents; 4) the documents may have untapped historical significance; and 5) certain kinds of documents are very attractive. In the paragraphs below I discuss these five elements in greater detail.

Until recently, the collectibles marketplace largely ignored historical western documents. These were left to institutions such as libraries, historical societies, and museums, and few private parties developed this hobby.

During the 1980s, however, many new collectors entered the marketplace as interest in western Americana inexplicably began to accelerate. Values and trading activity increased for

```
                            4002 West Seventeenth St.,
                            Los Angeles, California,
                            June 8, 1928.

Mr. Stuart N. Lake,
3916 Portola Place,
San Diego, California.

Dear Mr. Lake:

        Mrs. Earp and I are now returned from the
desert; we have been home for about a week and we
are glad to be back.

        Now I realize that it is beginning to be
vacation time, and while I do not know what you have
in mind for the summer, if it is at all coincident
with your plans, I shall be pleased to have you call
to see me; we shall be here until Fall.

        If you should drive out, please let me sug-
gest that you select either Sixteenth Street or Wash-
ington (Nineteenth) Street in traveling west through
the city (as Seventeenth Street is not cut through),
as far west as Ninth Avenue, then to Seventeenth Street
and thence east for a block. The street car service is
convenient over the Sixteenth (red) car line or the
Washington St. ("W" - yellow) car line.

        Mrs. Earp and I shall look for you; we trust
you are well and we send you the kind regards.

                            Very sincerely,

                            Wyatt S. Earp.
```

Wyatt Earp died six months after writing this 1928 letter to Stuart Lake, a journalist who agreed to rewrite Earp's autobiography. At eighty, the broke and destitute lawman from Tombstone, then living in Los Angeles, still hoped to earn an income from his life story but could not find a publisher. Lake's version was published several years later.

such items as historical autographs, obsolete stocks and bonds, old postal pieces, diaries, maps, photographs, and other varied documents. These individual collecting fields sometimes merge—as when finding an autograph on a stock certificate, or a revenue stamp on a photograph. But all these collectibles generally fall under the category of paper Americana.

The fact that this collecting field has been overlooked for so long is certainly an advantage to new collectors. Rare western documents commonly remain available to average collectors today. This situation, of course, will not last forever. Common-grade material will almost always be available, but the rare pieces eventually will end up changing hands only at auctions or through private trading.

Usually common-grade western documents on the collector's market are priced appropriately, but rare documents have been undervalued for many years. This is mainly because many paper Americana dealers lack the knowledge or appraisal skills to determine a document's true value, and this applies to autographed western documents as well.

Most paper Americana dealers or auction houses tend to deal in many types of paper collectibles. Since western documents comprise only a small part of their overall inventory, the dealers or autioneers may not be familiar with market prices that fluctuate with collector demand. It is difficult for them to be knowledgeable in all forms of paper collectibles. This is a great advantage to collectors. Many dealers don't take the time or have the resources to adequately study the content or signatures of the documents in their possession. Dozens of times during the 1980s I have bought documents for a fraction of their real value.

One collector of paper currency and coinage who recently expanded his collecting interests expressed amazement at the fantastic prices of some early western documents; considering their historical value, they were so affordable. He had been accustomed to paying hundreds or thousands of dollars for rare items in his regular collecting field.

Western paper Americana is a unique collecting field. Thousands of documents of the same type generally do not exist, as is usually the case with coins or stamps. Many historical western documents are very scarce because they were not mass manufactured or printed. Some exist only as "one of a kind."

Many items on today's market are obviously manufactured collectibles. Both the historical value and the return on your investment are bound to be low when you buy one of those widely advertised, mass-produced collector's plates. The fine print in the ads might say "only 10,000 available" or "limited to 100 firing days," but mass production of these technically "limited editions" lessens their uniqueness. Other examples of limited editions, such as new baseball cards, art prints, "silver" collectibles, and so on, are more likely to profit the producers than the collectors, and should be avoided.

Historical western documents are usually rare, single-piece items at least ninety years old. They are not modern reproductions. In many cases they were not mass produced. They capture the essence of life as it happened during the exploration and colonization of the West.

With the slow but sure decay of many early western mining camps, railroad towns, stagecoach stations, military posts, and ranches, historical documents are one of the few tangible items that remain as proof of their material existence. As such, these documents capture moments of time in western history, allowing modern collectors to experience the lingering aura of the Old West.

Most documents from the days of exploration and colonization in western history were destroyed many years ago. Hundreds of sites in the early West boomed suddenly; but many

POST OF FORT KEOGH, MONTANA,

November 16th 1885

COPY TELEGRAM.

Adjutant General
Fort Snelling Minn.

Major Snyder informs me by courier that he is confident from what he can learn that all is quiet on the Tongue and Rosebud rivers; but to investigate the matter more fully he has personally gone with an escort of one Officer and four men of 5th Infantry to Agency. He has ordered Capt. Edgerly's Troop back to this post and they will arrive to day.

(Signed) Wilkins – Comdg.

Official copy respectfully furnished.

Chas. P. Thompson
1st Lieutenant and Adjutant 5th Infantry,
Post Adjutant.

This telegram from the commanding officer Wilkins at Fort Keogh, Montana Territory, attests to lingering Indian troubles in the mid-1880s. Sent to the adjutant general at Fort Snelling, Minnesota, it reports "that all is quiet on the Tongue and Rosebud rivers, but to investigate the matter more fully [Major Snyder] has personally gone with an escort of one officer and four men of the 5th Infantry to the [Indian] Agency. He has ordered Capt. Edgerly's troops back to this post and they will arrive today."

busted suddenly, too, and when they did their records and papers often disappeared with the settlements. Fires ravaged nearly every early community, large and small alike, at least once—if not two or three times—and frequently these fires also ravaged their public and private records.

Few of the documents that survived these kinds of destruction end up on the market, and some get thrown away, even today. I know of several instances where preservation-minded individuals have scavenged important historical documents from dumps. Such finds may be old courthouse records or personal papers cleaned out of an attic after the death of an elderly person. The adage "one man's trash is another man's treasure" certainly applies to this unique collecting field.

The sad truth is that many old documents are gone forever, but, occasionally, a previously unknown collection turns up. That's very exciting. An astute collector must constantly evaluate documents on the market, searching for the rare, important nuggets among them.

Collecting old documents is a hobby, but collecting rare, historic documents is a hobby with investment value. Collectors must learn to distinguish the hobby from the investment. A document with important content or one that is signed by a famous Westerner is going to be highly prized by the knowledgeable collector.

On several occasions I have bought documents from large collections or in large groups. These usually contain the personal papers of someone important and may eventually contribute to a biography or other book because they reveal the writer's insights, opinions, and views. Owning letters and papers written or signed by men and women who played roles in developing

As some mining companies were indeed dubious, others owned mines with riches beyond anyone's imagination. Such was the case of the Little Pittsburg Mine of Leadville, Colorado, which made millionaires of David Moffat, Horace Tabor, and Jerome Chaffee. Moffat and Chaffee used profits from the Little Pittsburg to make their fortunes; Tabor died a pauper.

the West allows you to share in the thoughts, actions, joys, and sorrows through the documents.

The only thing more exciting than finding historic documents is finding *attractive* historic documents. Printing companies often adorned official papers and certificates with illustrations. The artwork on stocks and bonds usually reflects the type of industry of the business issuing them. A mining stock, for instance, might illustrate miners working in a shaft; a railroad bond may show a smoking locomotive pulling a passenger train through the mountains; a stock from an oil company might portray an oil field spouting a gusher.

Any historical document with visual appeal is more desirable than one without it. Attractive documents often cross a collector's path, but to find one that is both beautiful and historically valuable is a special discovery.

Financial documents are often quite attractive. Certificates for stocks and bonds rate highest among western documents in terms of beauty and elegance because they are usually printed in several colors and have handsome artwork. Checks, bank drafts, and certificates of deposits may also be pleasing to the eye. Letterheads, commissions, appointments, billheads, and broadsides are other examples of documents that sometimes have fancy illustrations. The most

The discovery of oil in Texas at Spindletop set off a new kind of gold rush in the West—the search for black gold. The petroleum industry was slow to develop primarily due to the lack of transportation, distribution, and refineries. Still, Spindletop sparked a new commitment in the West to search for oil and gas. Within two years of the original discovery, some 200 "oil companies" were selling Spindletop stock regardless of whether they were producing oil. Newspaper editorials called the region "Swindletop." This 1901 stock's vignette features a bird's-eye view of the company's oil fields.

attractive documents are usually printed by a bank note company or by the federal government's Bureau of Engraving and Printing within the Treasury department.

The illustrations on old documents may be of buildings, portraits, animals, floral designs, patriotic scenes, eagles, mythical figures, or outdoor scenes such as mountains, skylines, and harbors. The steel-plate engravings of a century ago were meticulously and painstakingly etched by hand, sometimes taking months to complete. The technique is nearly a lost art form. Only a handful of living experts can produce engravings in this manner, and these individuals usually work for a bank note company or the Bureau of Engraving and Printing—or they're serving time in prison for counterfeiting!

Documents illustrated with intricate artwork and printed in vivid colors increase the collector value, and select pieces from a collection are sometimes framed and displayed so they can be easily seen and enjoyed. I exhibit about twenty pieces from my collection in both my home and office, and visitors always notice them and comment on their beauty.

The energizing aspect of this dynamic collecting field is being able to own genuinely rare or unique documents that link us to the past. You can own and care for pieces of history that helped shape the American West. No other copies exist. The rarity varies from one document to another, and the knowledge you gather helps determine the scarcity of each piece.

To know and understand the marketplace where historical western documents are bought and sold is crucial. One way to get started is by getting on the mailing lists of dealers who offer catalogs. Attending collectible shows, subscribing to paper collectibles publications, and joining related organizations also helps.

The degree of commitment and involvement in the marketplace varies among individual collectors. But the more knowledgeable you become, the better your chances of maximizing your collection potential. Being involved is part of the collector's lifestyle.

Demand for western paper Americana will always exceed supply. As collector ranks swell, prices for high-quality documents will increase—but so will the care these documents receive and their chances of survival for future generations to learn from and enjoy.

The Paper Chase: Where to Find Old Documents

Where does one find old documents? This is what newcomers to the field of western paper Americana want to know. Some dealers regard the answer as a trade secret. Really it's just a matter of understanding the marketplace and learning how to tap into it. Still, one of the more exciting ways to find old documents is by stumbing upon them while exploring abandoned homesteads or ghost towns.

I distinctly remember my second encounter with old documents, in 1973, the year after I found the old shoebox containing papers and dynamite. I was with my brother Tim at a coal-mining ghost town called Spring Canyon near Price, Utah. The abandoned buildings stood in the mouth of a narrow canyon. The fence separating them from the road was clearly posted:

PRIVATE PROPERTY—KEEP OFF TRESPASSERS WILL BE SHOT

Both of us were at the age where we knew better, but we couldn't resist the urge to explore the well-preserved ghost town. We parked in some nearby bushes and hiked around the fence to take some photographs and get a better look. Walking through the townsite was eerie; we felt like we had entered an episode of the "Twilight Zone." Many of the homes and businesses were furnished; everything seemed dusty and old but strangely intact. It was as if the citizens of the community had simply vanished many years before, leaving everything behind. The wooden filing cabinets in the dentist's office still held old dental records, and other drawers stored his tools. A large safe on rollers at the bank sat partially opened, exposing numerous bank and insurance papers.

Suddenly shots rang out, shattering our silent exploration and providing a sobering reminder that we were on private property.

I decided to return to our car but didn't get far before an irate, rifle-toting rancher confronted me. He accused me of looting and began berating me with words I seldom heard in Utah. I apologized profusely and assured him that I had taken only pictures with my camera, but it did no good. He threatened to shoot me if I ever came back. I got his message and didn't return to Spring Canyon for twelve years. By then, the ghost town had disappeared. The entire site had been bulldozed, and dense brush reclaimed the canyon's mouth.

Although it's still possible to find old documents in remote corners of the West, collectors should always respect the rights of property owners and avoid trespassing. There are easier (and less dangerous) ways to find documents. It's just a matter of knowing where to begin. New collectors can get involved in the document marketplace in a number of ways. Listed here are ten places or means to acquire documents:

Dealer/Auction Catalogs: Since both dealers and collectors are scattered throughout the country, the best thing you can do as a collector is subscribe to catalogs offered by dealers and auction firms. Receiving the catalogs at your home allows you to study the offerings and buy or place bids at your convenience. The cost of subscribing is offset by this practical way to stay in touch with the marketplace.

Periodical Publications: Collectors can also subscribe to a variety of both general and specialized publications and magazines. While general publications cover mainstream antiques and collectibles, specialty publications focus on specific collecting fields. Subscribing to several publications of this type keeps you abreast of current news and information and helps you learn about the marketplace and the networks that brings collectors and dealers together. Some books are also available on specific collecting fields.

Collecting/Historical Organizations: Selecting and joining a few organizations is another good way to meet other collectors and dealers who share your interests. Most organizations hold annual (or other regular) meetings and offer their members informative newsletters in which they announce shows and print related advertisements. Becoming a member is a good way to get acquainted with a particular collecting field.

Collectibles Shows: Urban areas usually host collectibles shows. Some shows focus specifically on paper Americana; others target a broader collectibles market. A paper Americana show could yield some interesting finds, but experience has taught me that shows featuring antiques seldom offer documents or other forms of paper Americana.

Coin, Stamp, and Book Shows: These exhibitions often bring dealers and collectors from several states together under one roof, increasing your chances of finding worthwhile collectibles. Watch for ads in major newspapers or in other collecting publications and make a point of attending.

Coin, Stamp, and Book Shops: Some of these businesses carry various forms of documents, letters, stock certificates, and other papers as part of their inventory. Identify the stores in your area and check to see what they offer.

Antique/Collectibles Shops: My experience in checking at these shops over the years reveals that few of them handle documents. Yet, once in a while you'll run across a shop that deals with all types of paper Americana. Finding one usually requires some patient searching, but they do exist.

Flea Markets: Don't underestimate the value of these. You never know when someone might pull a box of old papers out of an attic somewhere and sell them at the flea market. I have found some good collectibles at great prices at flea markets. Attend these whenever possible.

Advertisements: Some collectors and dealers take out ads in newspapers and trade publications such as collectibles magazines or association newsletters. Often these state what the advertiser is looking for, but they may also offer an item for sale. Either way, it's another means of getting collectors, dealers, and private parties together. Running small advertisements in local newspapers has produced some of my best finds.

Estate Sales: These common events take place when someone dies, leaving the person's relatives or others responsible parties to dispose of the personal property of the deceased. Usually estate sales consist of property and household furnishings, but occasionally a box or two of personal papers may be included. Personal papers in this case may also include old letters, legal documents, and so forth that belonged to other family members who preceded the deceased in death. Contact the estate sale auctioneer to ask if any personal papers will be offered.

Whether you live in a rural or urban area, the above suggestions can put you in touch with the collectibles marketplace. Balancing your participation between subscribing to catalogs, joining associations, and attending various shows and shops will get you started in the right direction.

CHAPTER TWO
Evaluating Documents

Once you have determined to start your own collection, you need to learn how to effectively evaluate the documents you might want to buy. The experience you'll eventually gain through patience and practice may enable you to develop a "feel" for examining old documents. Meanwhile, though, you have to rely on evaluating documents by learning about their key components —paper, printing, and ink—and examining various aspects that affect the desirability of any particular historical western document.

Paper manufacturing. The manufacture of paper in the United States began about 1700, with the establishment of the first American paper mill in Pennsylvania. Demand was limited in those days, but it increased, and by 1800 there were about fifty paper mills in the U.S., most of them in Pennsylvania. The Industrial Revolution mechanized the paper-making process by the 1830s, quickly replacing the slow, laborious hand-produced methods.

Handmade papers of the 1700s and early 1800s were made from cotton, linen, and other cloth-type rags. These materials produced a strong, durable, fine-grade of paper; however, to meet the increasing demand for paper, machine-manufactured paper mills turned to wood pulp as a substitute to cloth. Wood pulp made paper faster and cheaper.

The process made paper more widely available at a lower cost, but its overall quality decreased. Unlike their cloth-based counterparts, papers made from wood pulp tend to have shorter fibers and more natural acids, which act to break down the paper over time and also accounts for acid-related discolorations, brittleness, and deterioration along the edges. As a compromise, some manufacturers produced paper from a blend of rag-type materials and wood pulp. Printers generally produced shorter-term documents (invoices and receipts, for instance) on inexpensive paper and reserved the higher grade rag paper for longer-term important financial or government-related documents.

Paper manufacturers often incorporate watermarks—translucent impressions—into their product. When you hold these papers up to a bright light, you'll be able to see the watermark. Usually it tells the name of the paper mill and its location; sometimes the impression is of a trademark or even a date. The practice of using watermarks began around 1830 and continues today. Watermarks are not to be confused with water stains, which detract from a document's appearance and value.

Documents from the early period of the American West, the 1840s and 1850s, were commonly printed on light blue or white paper and were very simple in design. Typically the extent of pre-printing on these documents, if any, was limited to the printer's name, date, and location, leaving blanks for other information to be filled in by hand. By the 1860s and 1870s, however, improved printing methods led to the creation of more attractive documents, many of which displayed ornate vignettes; this practice continued beyond the turn of the century.

Printers. Documents from the Old West may have been printed right in the communities where they were issued or may have come from many miles away. Printers may be classed at three levels: 1) local or community printers, such as those at Marysville (California), Eureka (Utah), or Hays (Kansas); 2) regional printers, such as those at Albuquerque, Denver, or Butte; and 3) national printers, such as those in New York, St. Louis, or San Francisco.

Occasionally printers identify their business in very small letters near the bottom of the document—this is an "imprint." As you might expect, documents printed by small community shops are generally harder to obtain than those printed by regional or national operations.

Financial documents printed by regional or national printers are among the most attractive documents available to collectors of paper Ameri-

This 1888 mining stock from Deadwood, Dakota Territory, exemplifies the multiple business talents of lawman Seth Bullock, who signed it as president of the mining company. Previously a lawman in Montana Territory, Bullock came to Deadwood on the heels of the Black Hills gold rush and became its first sheriff. He promptly arrested Wild Bill Hickok's killer and turned Deadwood into a respectable community. He owned several businesses in the Black Hills, where he also ran a large ranch and dabbled in mining. A long-standing friendship with Teddy Roosevelt assured Bullock's appointment as U.S. marshal by the president.

cana. Large companies that printed important financial documents, such as currency, checks, and stocks and bonds, among other things, were usually called "bank note" printers. Several major bank note companies still provide this service today.

Stock certificates, bonds, and other important documents printed by bank note companies have a characteristic look and feel that qualify them as distinctly superior documents. Such documents are often ornate, with handsome titles and detailed vignettes (illustrations) printed in bold colors. These documents were usually printed on 25 percent rag paper, giving them the texture and crispness of new currency. The paper was manufactured specifically to ensure durability from the everyday handling and usage of these documents.

Although ornate documents look and feel great, there's another reason for printing financial documents in this manner. Counterfeiting and document alterations became a growing problem by the mid-1800s, and printers were motivated to devise new ways to reduce the occurrence of fraud. Adorning documents with fancy borders and company titles soon became standard, then adding more meticulous detailing and vignettes provided the issuing institutions extra security.

Printing company engravers applied their craft on copper, and later steel, plates. Illustrations of industrial scenes, landscapes, buildings, railroads, and miners soon appeared on a growing number of financial documents. These highly detailed scenes were painstakingly etched onto the metal plates, sometimes taking weeks or months to finish. The combined use of a quality paper, bolder printing colors, ornate vignettes, patterns, and borders became an effective obstacle to financial forgers.

Beyond this practical aspect lay a more subtle reason for incorporating artwork into the valuable documents. Psychologically, the vivid colors, bold titles, and beautiful illustrations created the feeling or sense of wealth and prosperity. They lent credence to the value of the documents and produced a feeling of success to those who held them. In essence, it assured the bearer that his investment was sound and secure.

A vignette of an active oil field—with flowing gushers, full storage tanks, and barrels brimming with oil ready for shipping—painted an optimistic future for the shareholder of an oil stock. The same effect is created on a bank draft or certificate of deposit through a vignette of a four-story bank building on a busy street corner. The engravings and artwork became more ornate over the years. By the early 1900s anything less than the fine detail produced by a bank note company just wouldn't do for important financial documents.

The American Bank Note Company, which still exists today, outgrew all of its contemporaries. It incorporated in 1858 through the consolidation of several major eastern printers. Although other eastern printers also produced attractive western financial documents, the bank note companies listed below dominated the business between 1860 and 1920.

- Columbia Bank Note Company
- Franklin Bank Note Company
- Hamilton Bank Note Company
- Homer Lee Bank Note Company
- International Bank Note Company
- John Lowell Bank Note Company
- National Bank Note Company
- Republic Bank Note Company
- Security Bank Note Company
- Union Bank Note Company
- Western Bank Note Company
- E. A. Wright Bank Note Company

Printers of western documents sometimes made typographical or historical errors, as the New York Bank Note Company did on this 1908 Western Nevada Copper stock. It says the company was "incorporated under the laws of the State of Arizona," but that territory did not become a state until 1912.

In addition to these giants, several western printers also left their imprint on important documents. Some examples of these are:

- Britton & Rey, San Francisco
- John Partridge, San Francisco
- Towne & Bacon, San Francisco
- Crocker & Company San Francisco
- Collier/Cleveland Litho, Denver
- The Denver Litho Company, Denver
- Utah Litho, Salt Lake City
- Tribune Print, Salt Lake City
- Gast Bank Note, St. Louis
- St. Louis Bank Note Company, St. Louis
- Rhodes & Allen, Kansas City
- Goes Company, Chicago

Obviously, the most important printers in the early West based their operations in major cities. They commonly produced documents for use in distant territories and states. However, many of the more common-type documents do not include the printer's name.

This certificate ordained a Mormon to the office of a "Seventy." The stamped signature of Seymour Young, a son of Brigham, appears with that of the controversial and colorful J. Golden Kimball.

This early Colorado Territory mining document, staking claim to Calhoun Lode near Central City, features attractive vignettes and a revenue tax stamp. It is signed by J. Frederick Pierson, a Civil War general who was captured and imprisoned at Libby. After the war he crossed the plains to Colorado and started a career in mining.

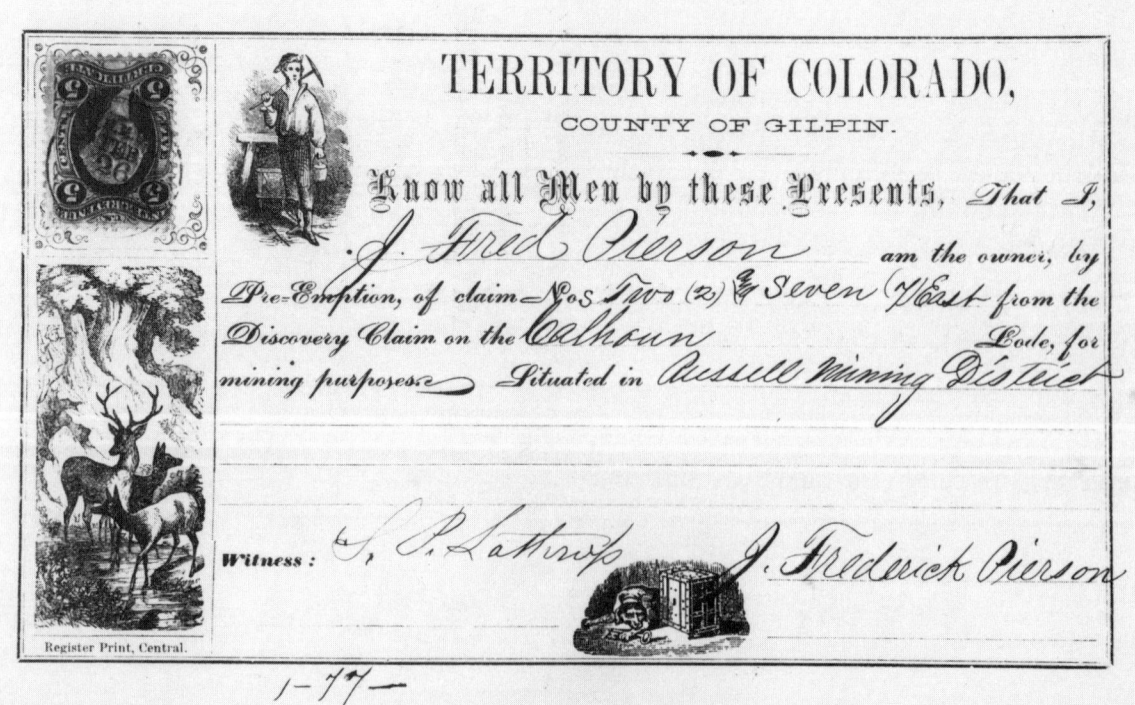

Inks and pens. The earliest inks produced for public use in the United States were made from either carbon or a combination of iron and tree galls. The basic formula called for grinding tree galls into powder, purifying it with rain water, then straining it and adding gum arabic, copper or iron crystals, and sugar. While useful, the ink made from iron and galls produced a by-product of sulfuric acid, which, when dripped or globbed on paper, eventually burned holes in those spots.

This type of ink was used mostly with feather quills, the standard writing instrument through the early 1800s. During the mid-1800s steel-nibbed pens and other experimental designs, such as the tips of animal horns, diamonds and other gemstones, and even gold-plated and glass tips, were tried. But these all still required frequent dipping into an inkwell. Then, in the late 1800s, fountain pens emerged as the best alternative to the constant dipping. With the improved technology came a demand for a more compatible ink, one that flowed well from the pen's nib. Dyes and other less-corrosive ingredients replaced ink made from iron and tree galls and improved the flow of ink from the reservoir pens, which remained the instrument of choice until ball-point pens came along during World War II.

Of course, the pen's major competitor over the years was the lead or graphite pencil. Most people favored pencils because they performed reliably and weren't messy. A sizeable portion of the letters written by soldiers during the Civil War were written with pencils. Unlike inks and pens, pencils have undergone few improvements over the last century or two; most of the changes are in the design of the pencil itself, the introduction of erasers, and the refinement of the pencil's use.

Some Tips on Evaluating Documents

New collectors sometimes ask what I look for when I'm deciding whether to buy or pass up an available document. Before buying any document I scrutinize it carefully for clues to help me determine its value. Each document has a number of elements worthy of scrutiny, and these vary in importance according to what type of document you are examining.

Listed here are ten factors that help me determine the value and desirability of a document, including the type of document, its place of origin, its date or age, its attractiveness, what subject or category it fits into, its content, its condition, whether it bears a printer identification, any signatures or autographic value, and its overall rarity or collection value. It's important to weigh these factors both individually and collectively to help you understand the historical value of any given document.

Type of document. One of the things collectors must determine is the type of document before them. Is it a letter? A telegram? A commission? A check? Certain types of documents, such as letters or certificates for stocks and bonds, may generate more interest among collectors than items such as receipts or invoices. Some people limit their collections to one or only a few types of documents, while others want anything based on a specific subject. The chapter on building your collection discusses more about the types of documents you might want in relation to the subject matter.

My Dear Lorenzo,
Kindly pass this letter to Daniel S. Parker
As Always Bob Parker

Lander Wyoming March 13, 1890

My Dear Brother,

It has been so long since I have written I suppose you have almost done looking for a letter from me but do not despair for you shall have one after so long a time you must forgive me for not writing before I have no excuse to offer only my negligence and I will try to be more punctual for the future. I was very sorry to hear that you are in hidding again, but you know that I am not one to point a finger only be carefull for I am inclined to think as Grand father Parker did about the wild cat in Duncan woods. I do wish I could come and see you all and I intend to if nothing happens to prevent this Summer coming for I almost feel homesick when thinking how long it is since I saw my Mother it seems almost an age since I saw any of you. When you get this letter you must write me and tell me all the news and what the prospects are for a safe reunion I hope we may have a grand revelry but I should think it doubtful according to your letter. I am now located at a good house about 12 miles from Lander and have taken to raising horses which I think suits this country just fine. H— and I have throwed our lots entirely together so we have 38 horses between us and we would have more but it has been a cold winter with plenty of snow and wind. (and you must excuse the pencile but the ink froze.) Business here is very dull and money hard but you know I am well. I should be in perfect health if I did not have such a good appitite and eat so much 3 times each day I must close my letter

Hiding from the law near Lander, Wyoming Territory, after a series of train and bank robberies, Robert LeRoy Parker, alias Butch Cassidy, wrote this letter to his brother, Daniel, who was also in hiding at their uncle's farm in Parowan, Utah, after holding up a stagecoach. Butch apologized for not writing more

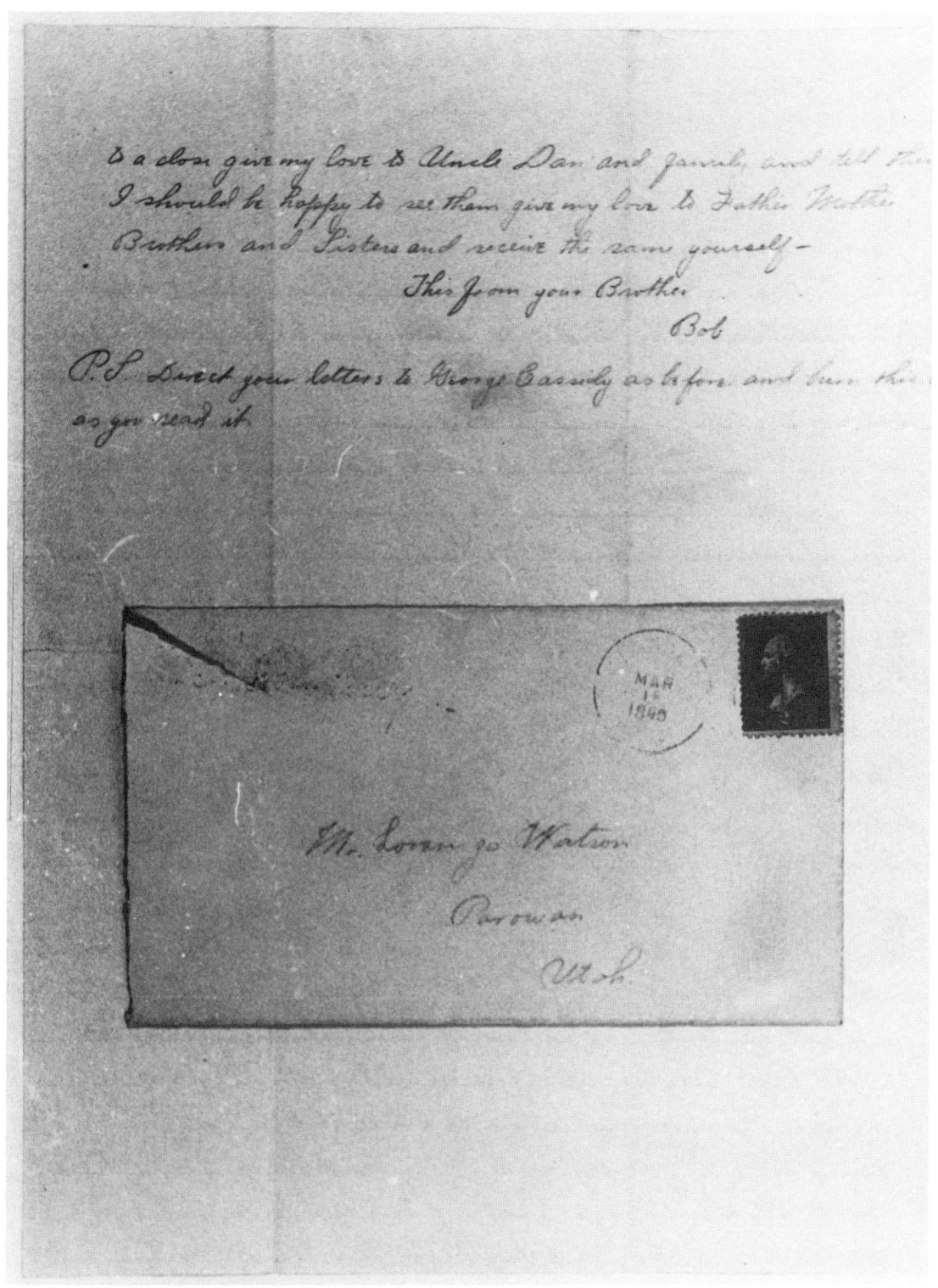

often, adding, "I was very sorry to hear that you are in hiding again, but you know that I am not one to point a finger...." Daniel Parker was soon caught and imprisoned; later he became a law enforcement officer in Utah. What happened to Butch in later years remains a mystery and continues to stir lively debates among historians.

—21—

Place of origin. Documents from some areas of the West are harder to find than those from other areas, depending on when the document was created and how many people lived there at the time. Although many documents identify their place of origin, some make no mention of a state or territory. Quite a few once-thriving settlements have either long since ceased to exist or changed their names. When confronted with situations like this, reference books, libraries, or state historical societies may help you solve the mystery. Try to avoid documents with no place name or clues to their place of origin.

Date or age. As a rule of thumb, the oldest documents are usually the least common and, therefore, most desirable. Collectors generally strive to acquire older, scarcer items. Western documents from the 1850s and 1860s are hardest to find, especially if they aren't from large cities. Those from the 1870s and 1880s may be rare if they originated in sparsely settled regions. With a few exceptions, your objective should be to collect as much as possible from the nineteenth century. As you attend collectors' shows and look through dealers' catalogs, pay attention to how the age of a document affects its value.

Dates and places intersect very precisely, and together they can tell you much about a document's collector value. To illustrate this, let's assume you can afford to buy only one of two available land grants—one from California and one from Montana Territory—both dated in 1870. Which would you choose? In 1870 California had about thirty times the population of

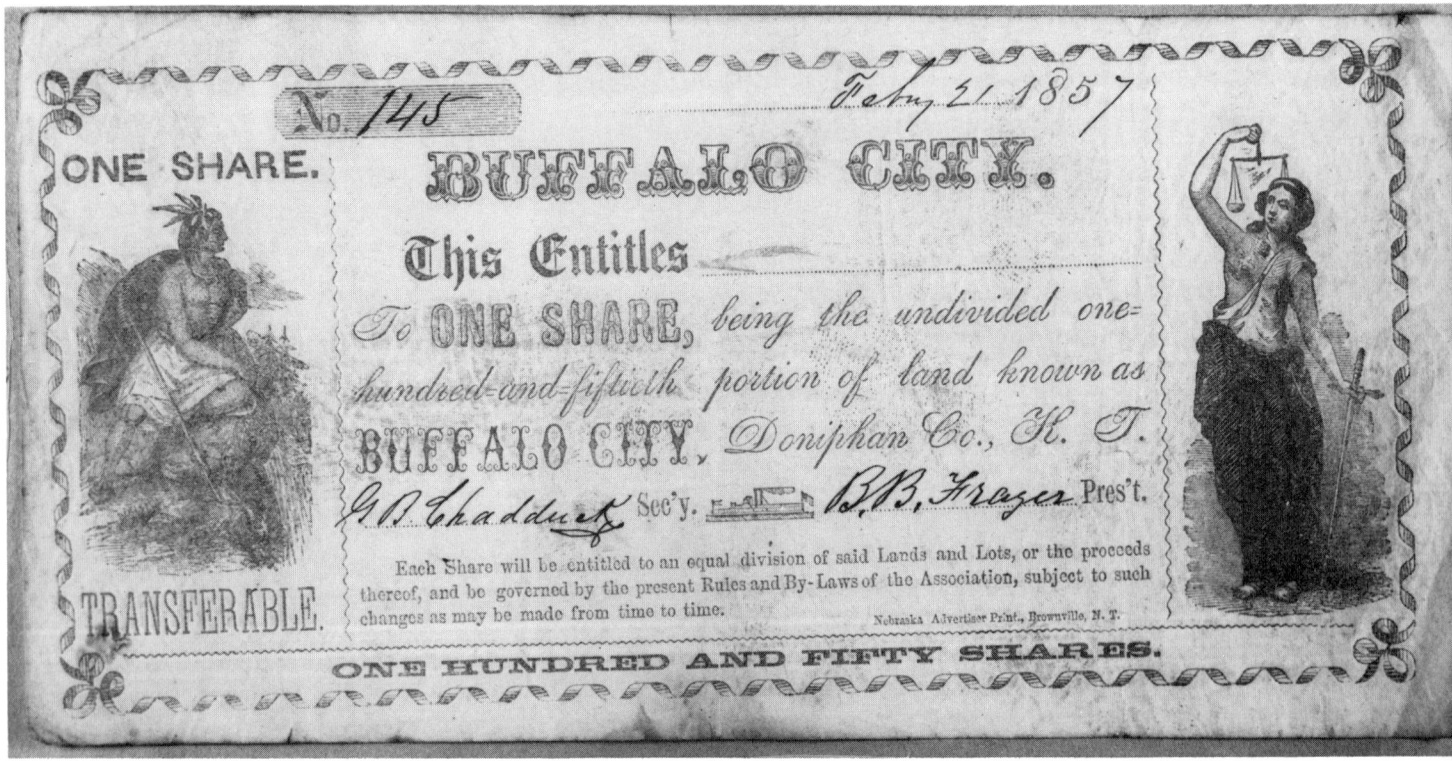

Early promoters of land development sometimes formed townsite companies to encourage settlement. This 1857 Kansas Territory stock is the oldest of its kind I have seen for sale. It is issued for one share, representing 1/150th of the available land. Research on Buffalo City reveals little information, suggesting the community vanished with its namesake.

Montana. Fewer people means fewer documents, so the Montana grant would be more valuable than the one from California.

Attractiveness. Collectors are naturally drawn to visually appealing collectibles, and the price usually reflects this. Western documents vary greatly in their appearance: some are plain, perhaps entirely handwritten and totally devoid of artwork; others are semi-illustrated, perhaps with a title printed at the top and a simple border design; still others are ornate, displaying intricate, colorful artwork and one or more elaborate illustrations. The documents may be printed in one or more colors on high-grade paper or vellum. Bear in mind that the price of many nice pieces is incorrectly based largely on their attractiveness, regardless of the document's historical value or the quantity in existence.

Subject or category. Nearly all documents are directly or indirectly associated with some aspect of business or government. Law enforcement, banking, mining, railroads, cattle, and military documents are among the most popular categories with western paper Americana collectors, many of whom build their collections around one or several of these subjects. A letterhead from a mining company will command a higher price than one from a hardware store.

Content. All documents warrant close examination for content. This is one of the most important elements to evaluate, and your knowledge of history could help you determine whether a given document is priced appropriately. A military paper signed by George Custer might sell for a few thousand dollars, but a handwritten letter by him could sell for much more. You'll learn more about this crucial element in Chapter Four.

Condition. A document's overall condition reflects the treatment it has received over the years. If it has been folded, spilled on, left lying in the sun, or been subjected to various other forms of negligent handling, the result is bound to show. Even the type of paper and ink used in printing can determine how well a document ages. Some documents look and feel clean and fresh, as if they were printed just yesterday; others show a bit of wear and tear; still others look fully tattered and torn. The document's condition certainly affects its value.

Printer. Some documents bear the printer's name near the bottom of the paper. Printer identification doesn't always affect the document's value, but those printed by a bank note company are usually worth more than those printed elsewhere.

Signatures or autographic value. Most of the documents collectors encounter are signed by someone. Some signatures are legible; others are not. Some people signed only with an "X." A signature can add to a document's selling price—if the seller realizes the autographic value. Some of the best surprises I've had in my years collecting paper Americana have been finding autographed documents by important yet little-known Westerners. I acquired about half of the autographed items in my collection from people who didn't recognize the autographic value. In some cases I, too, didn't know what I had until later discovering it through research.

Overall rarity. Usually by the time you've evaluated the areas already mentioned, you'll have a good idea about a document's rarity and collector value. With practice you'll learn how to consider all these elements in less than a minute.

Always study the document as a whole and in all its various parts, then apply your analysis against the seller's price. Avoid using the price as your guide. Ask questions to clarify any doubt you might have about a document before you buy it, and beware of sellers who can't or won't answer your questions satisfactorily.

Revered as one of the West's most infamous outlaws, Jesse James reveals kindness and humanity in this handwritten letter, which reads: "You have always been so faithful. For all your goodness I give you my thanks forever. The horses were among the best. Never were deserters. I hope the best of luck will be yours and that someday everything can be restored to you. I will always remember our [Civil] war days together. Faithfully we fought for a cause. Fought for the rights of many of our good people up and down the country. Some of us have begun life anew. Some of us were never officially surrendered. Some of us have been outlawed—only God can know are hearts. Again I give you my many thanks. Most sincerely, Jesse James." James was killed two years later by Bob Ford, a member of his own gang, for the reward money.

—24—

CHAPTER THREE

Autographs

Discovering and collecting western autographs is one of the most exciting and enjoyable aspects of my involvement with historical western documents. Signatures of famous Westerners have become popular among autograph collectors, and this trend is reflected by the spiraling prices the autographs command. A signed photo of Geronimo that sold for $13,000 and a stock certificate signed by Buffalo Bill Cody that brought over $8,000 at auction confirm the increasing surge of interest in autographs.

One recent autograph dealer's catalog offered several choice western autographs to collectors willing to pay the price: $6,500 for a pair of documents signed by Virgil Earp as tax collector of Tombstone; $2,000 for a signed copy of a book by outlaw Emmett Dalton; $2,750 for a legal document signed by Sheriff Pat Garrett; $4,250 for another legal document signed by Judge Roy Bean; and $900 for a sworn oath of office signed by "Hanging Judge" Issac Parker.

There are two distinct price ranges that most western autographs fall into: $100-$1,000 and $1,000-$10,000. Autographs that start at four figures include those from well-known Westerners who left legacies—John Wesley Hardin, Wyatt Earp, Judge Roy Bean, Jesse James, George Custer, Pat Garrett, Kit Carson, and Geronimo, for example. The problem is that few collectors can afford to pay such high prices; even autographs in the lower price range represent an expensive purchase to the average collector.

Rarely will you encounter a document offered for its autographic value at less than $100. You may not always recognize the name, but you should never bypass a western autograph simply because it is unfamiliar to you. Base the merit of the autograph on the importance of the signer in relation to the type of document and its price. If you like the item, buy it. Hundreds of important Westerners played significant roles in the development of the West. Today's lesser-known names may be current sleepers at yesterday's prices for tomorrow's collectors.

The value of a western autograph is largely in the eye of the beholder. You should collect what you find interesting while remaining as close as you can to the mainstream of collecting. But any dealer or collector selling a western autograph should provide enough historical or biographical information to place the document in context and to accentuate its worth.

A collector from the East Coast called me some time ago asking for biographical information on several Mormon names I did not recog-

Written from Fort Cobb, Indian Territory, just days before its abandonment, George Custer wrote this letter to another military officer regarding his inability to pay soldiers due to the lack of blank pay accounts. Ironically, seven years before his own fate at the Little Big Horn, he said, "The Indian War is practically ended. All the hostile tribes have given themselves up or are en route to this post."

nize. The man had just returned from a book show where a dealer displayed several old documents signed by "important" Mormons who were "friends" of Joseph Smith. I checked my reference books. Nothing. The dealer offered no historical evidence or background information to support his claims about the documents, so I advised the collector to turn them down. Unfortunately, some dealers misuse words like "important" and "rare" without establishing any support or proof of the document's value.

One of the challenges in collecting western autographs is simply finding them for sale. Though the number of autograph dealers has tripled over the last decade, their offerings of western signatures remains sporadic. The reason is partly because of the difficulty in finding western autographs, but also because most dealer's recognize only a few dozen big names.

Wise collectors look beyond the limited offerings of autograph dealers. Since many types of documents received signatures, certain autographs may be found in other collecting fields. Signed stock certificates, for example, are available on the scripophily market as well as through autograph dealers. The same applies to old checks, currency, or books, all of which fall within their own organized collecting fields.

The autograph of an individual sometimes turns up in quantity, but not often. While this should affect the collector value, it doesn't always turn out that way; it depends on the person's importance, the quantity of autographs found, and what document bears the signature. For example, William F. Cody, or Buffalo Bill, was a prolific writer and autograph signer for nearly four decades. His signature is popular among "Old West" collectors. Yet, several groupings of his personal papers have surfaced on the autograph market since 1980, which temporarily "diluted" the market. Eventually, the demand catches up to the supply.

Some autographs are extremely hard to find while others show up repeatedly, depending upon which signatures you seek. With early western autographs you don't have the luxury of shopping among various dealers' catalogs because, unlike modern autographs, there aren't enough of the old signatures around to permit price comparisons

One indication a certain autograph exists in quantity is when several dealers offer it at differ-

The most recognizable of Montana's "Copper Kings," William Clark's spheres of influence in the West included mining, railroads, banking, and politics. He made millions from his copper mines in Montana and Arizona and served as a U.S. senator for six years, but those closest to him said bribery was Clark's specialty. Henry Allen, his right-hand man in Arizona who remained loyal for decades, eventually wrote a scathing exposé on Clark's illegal activities before commiting suicide, and Clark allegedly paid a newspaper publisher $10,000 to retrieve the story. Upon his death, in 1925, Clark's estate was worth over $25 million. This 1887 mining stock signed by Clark was issued to his banking firm, Clark and Larabie. Note the quality printing by the American Bank Note Company.

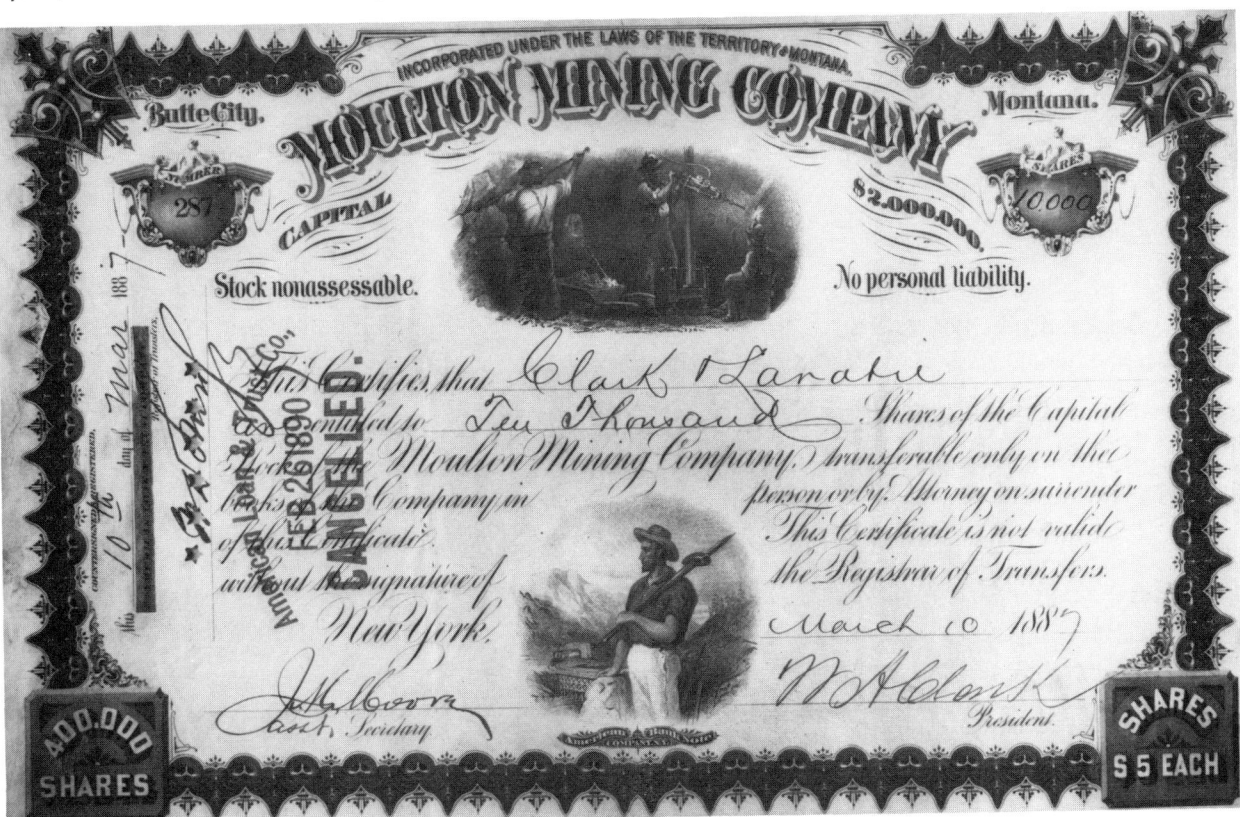

ent prices. Examples that immediately come to mind are western author Zane Grey's personal checks, Moulton Mining Company stocks signed by Montana Copper King and Senator William Clark, or Thomas Edison's business papers. However, unlike other areas of autograph collecting, western signatures are seldom available in large quantities. Usually just the opposite is true.

Research can reveal important clues as you investigate names and signatures. Your efforts could make the difference in simply owning a document or owning an *autographed* document. The results of your research can also dramatically change the value of a document, as illustrated by the following story.

In 1984 I bought several Wyoming oil stocks and filed them into my inventory. Several months later I pulled them out to list them for sale in an upcoming catalog. I glanced at the signatures on the stocks and heard a bell ring in the recesses of my mind. The shareholder on one of the stocks was "Joe La Fores."

Joe La Fores? *The* Joe La Fores? The famous Wyoming lawman? The man who chased Butch Cassidy and arrested Tom Horn? I caught my breath and quickly turned the certificate over. On the verso was his signature in green ink—Joe La Fores. But wait a minute ... the spelling didn't look right. Sure enough, the Wyoming lawman's name wasn't supposed to have an 'e'; it should have been Joe LaFors. My hopes dimmed. Still, the stock was issued from the lawman's home state. It was an itch I couldn't scratch. I had to find out.

Some collectors might have concluded it wasn't the right person when they saw that the signature on the back of the stock matched its spelling on the front. Had it been another type of document I might have done the same. But I knew from experience that if the name on a stock was misspelled, either the stock had to be voided and reissued, or the shareholder would be instructed to sign on the back (when redeeming it) exactly as his or her name had been spelled on the front.

I contacted the Western Heritage Center at the University of Wyoming and asked someone there to send me some samples of Joe LaFors' signature from the same time period; meanwhile, I sent them a photocopy of the signature from my stock. I soon received the evidence I needed to confirm that the signature I held was indeed that of *the* Joe LaFors—and very likely the only extant example where he purposefully misspelled his name.

My research paid off. And to think that I was ready to sell it for $20!

Many good western autographs still remain in the field to collect, but the rarest of pieces are rapidly disappearing from the marketplace. To seize opportunities when you meet them, you must act decisively. Indecision is perhaps the worst enemy of collectors. I can think of a number of instances where I stalled on buying a western autograph; by the time I decided to buy it, three or four collectors had already called the dealer—all wanting that one piece. I don't hesitate anymore, and neither should you if you're building a collection of western autographs.

You don't need a fat wallet or a degree in history to start collecting western autographs—just a desire to learn and enjoy what you learn. Start slow, be selective, and ask questions. Dwell on the reward (the autograph, its rarity, the joy of discovery) instead of the penalty (initial cost), and you'll be a smarter, happier collector.

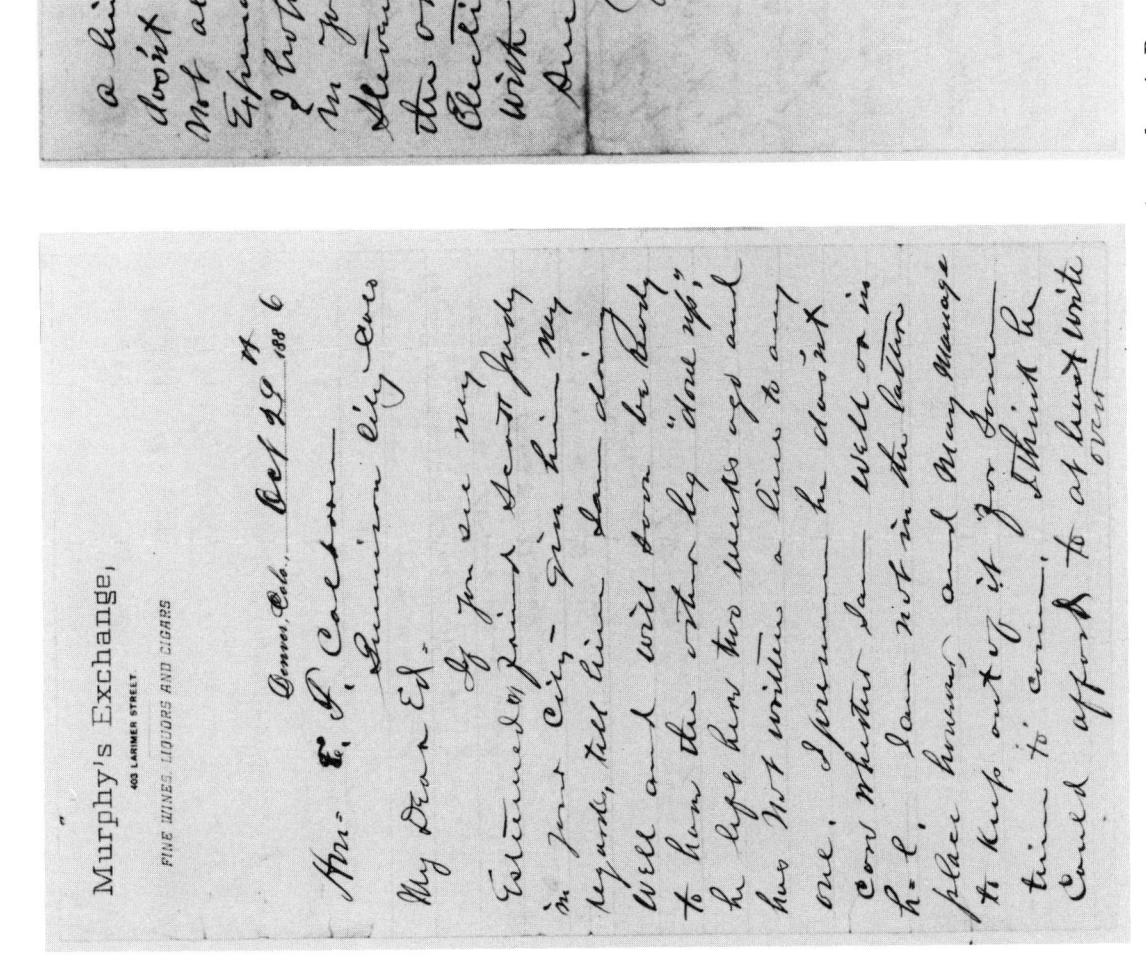

One of the West's most famous gamblers, W. B. "Bat" Masterson, sat in a saloon in Denver, Colorado, in the fall of 1886 and wrote this letter on the establishment's stationery. In it, Bat complains to one friend of not hearing from another, writing, "I presume he doesn't care whether I am well or in h--l. I am not in the latter place, however, and may manage to keep out of it for some time to come...."

Lawman Pat Garrett, hired as a private detective to solve the murder of Albert Fountain and his young son, wrote this hasty letter to his wife. It reads, in part: "I came in last night from a 7 day hunt for the body of Col. Fountain and his little boy, but failed to find anything, however, I have not given up and will start out again in a few days. It is only a matter of time when I will succeed. You know when I make up my mind to do anything I never quit . . ." Although their bodies were never found, Garrett's persistence led to the arrests of three men two years later. A jury found the trio not guilty, due to the lack of hard evidence. Garrett became famous about fifteen years earlier, when he killed Billy the Kid. In 1908 Garrett was shot by a business partner over a deal that had gone sour.

As members of Jesse James' outlaw gang, the Younger brothers—Cole, Bob, Jim, and John—were well trained in violence while growing up in Missouri during the Civil War. Cole rode with Quantrill's Raiders while his brothers fought with the Confederacy. After the Civil War the brothers turned to crime and eventually saddled up with Frank and Jesse James. Their downfall came at Northfield, Minnesota, in 1876, when local citizens thwarted the outlaws' attempt to rob the bank. All three Younger brothers were wounded and eventually captured. Cole spent the next 27 years in prison; he was pardoned in 1903. In this undated letter, possibly written from prison, Cole Younger told a friend in Texas: "I have spent some happy days in your town in Days long ago and hope to have the pleasure of again visiting the greatest of all states [Texas] and once more shake the hands of the old fellows that tromped down the bamboo [illegible word] and drove the red man back to the western plane. . . ."

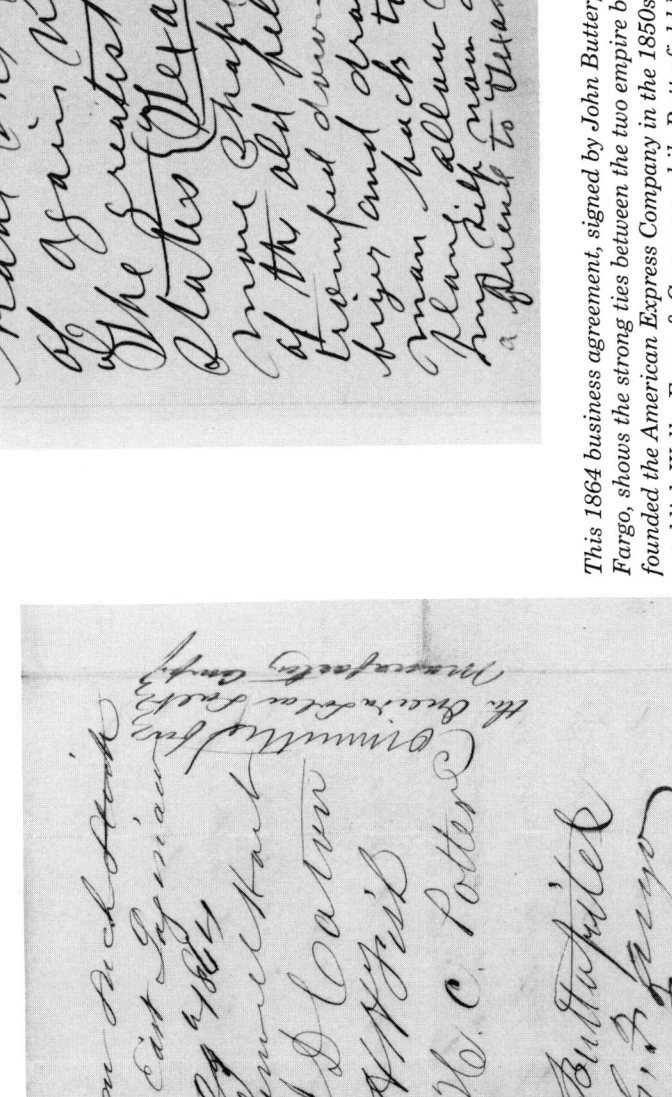

This 1864 business agreement, signed by John Butterfield and William and Charles Fargo, shows the strong ties between the two empire builders. Butterfield and Fargo founded the American Express Company in the 1850s. The Fargos later went on to establish Wells, Fargo & Company while Butterfield built the Overland Mail Company, both of which carried much of America's east-west mail during the 1850s and 1860s.

—31—

Serving as the first sheriff of Sacramento County, California, was no easy task for Ben McCulloch, despite his skills with a gun. After fighting for Texas independence in 1836, McCulloch served as one of the original Texas Rangers; he scouted first for "Captain Jack" Hays and continued as such during the Mexican War. He followed Hays to California during the gold rush and returned to Texas as a U.S. marshal after serving one term in California. During the Civil War he became a Confederate general and was killed at the Battle of Pea Ridge, Arkansas, in 1862.

As a rising star in New Mexico politics, Juan Patron had served the territory in numerous positions. As a deputy sheriff in 1878, during the Lincoln County War, Patron sided with the McSween faction and was shot in the back by John Riley of the Dolan-Murphy faction. He survived and became captain of the Lincoln County Rifles but was gunned down in a saloon six years later at the age of twenty-nine. The document shown is a certification received by Patron as sheriff for cattle brand markings.

Season of 1902.

From Buffalo Bill's Wild West.
A limited number of engagements only.

Annie Oakley.

Nutley 26th

My dear Friend.

Your kind xmas greeting rec'd It was worth more than A $ 50 one would have been to me. I thank you. Oh so much for your good kind wishes. I sent you a little card & letter to Deckertown I hope you will get it. With love and blessings for the New Year. from us both. I am Affect.'

Annie Oakley.

We will be here when you return. & & & if you are short dear. don't forget to let us know. it would be a pleasure for us to do you. A favor in any way. & &

Though not necessarily a figure of the Old West, Phoebe Ann Moses portrayed the "western girl" in the minds and hearts of thousands as "Annie Oakley," whose shooting skills as a youngster kept food on the family table. Over the years she honed her talent with a rifle and gained fame after outshooting marksman Frank Butler in a rifle match at the age of fifteen. Butler married her a year later, and the pair became one of the attractions of Buffalo Bill Cody's Wild West Show for many years. In this 1902 letter Oakley thanked a friend for sending a get-well card after being injured in a train crash. Note the vingette at the top of Oakley shooting at a target while riding a bicycle.

> New York 25th Sept 1889
>
> Colonel Henry E. Tremain.
>
> Colonel. I have received your Invitation on the part of the Veterans of the Seventh Regiment, National Guard, to be present with them at their Annual Dinner on the 7th of next month. It would have given me pleasure to join them but I have to regret that I shall not be in the city at the time of their dinner and have to beg you to make my acknowledgments for the courtesy of their invitation.
>
> Yours truly
> John C. Frémont

"Pathfinder" John C. Frémont is credited for numerous expeditions exploring the West during the 1840s and 1850s and for participating in the Bear Flag Revolt to gain California's independence from Mexico. He married Missouri Senator Thomas Hart Benton's daughter, Jessie, who helped her husband's fame by assisting in the writings of his expeditions. Frémont later served in the Civil War and became governor of Arizona Territory. In this 1889 letter from New York, Frémont declined an invitation to a military dinner.

CHAPTER FOUR

Content

Content can play a very important role in the value of a document. This struck me in a somber way while examining a new group of documents many years ago. I found an 1881 letter from Ottawa, Kansas, written on Missouri Pacific Railway Company letterhead. A son told his parents about the failing health of his wife. The letter read, in part:

Dear Parents

As I wrote in letter yesterday at Chamite, I write you now after seeing Mary. There is no possible chance for her recovery. She is liable to pass away at any time though probably several days and possibly weeks may elapse before the final hour shall come.

She is fully resigned to her departure and talks calmly of everything relating thereto— she wants, if possible for me to arrange to keep the children together as one family. Of course I shall do so if possible and it meets my views also. She will be buried at Quaker Street among her kindred and home.

She would like to see you very much and if you could come out it would be desireable. She went as far as to have the physician make out a telegram for you to come out—but he discreetly held it until my arrival. If one of you can come it would greatly please her very much. It is a sad hard thing to do to sit here in the room of my dying wife and write—I can not keep the scalding tears from my eyes—five months ago I wrote you of our excellent health—in that time I have been home twice and now for the final farewell.

The seeds of the insidious destroyer were there growing all unknown. She talks with the utmost calmness of death, believes it all ordained for the best—and gives advice in care of the children—what she wants done with them how she wants them brought up and where. She has made a memoranda distribution of articles and Mother Titus custodian of them for the children. More shortly.

Your Son,
A. C. Titus

I sat there quietly, reverently for a few moments trying to envision this scene and the difficulty A. C. Titus must have had in writing to his parents. Here was a vivid example of the real hardships early pioneers faced while colonizing the West: a young family with children, perhaps working forty acres and living in a crude cabin, the nearest doctor miles away. Harsh winters, poor health, little food. The combined elements often brought death in the spring across the West.

I set the letter aside and continued going through the group of documents, wondering what had happened to the family. Minutes later I found another letter A. C. Titus wrote to his parents dated nine days later. It read:

Dear Parents,

At 11:05 PM last night our dear Mary departed this life for the other. Her mental faculties free until a brief time before the final monent—not a struggle to the last—calmly breathing.

I read her your letter from you at noon. She said "I am so glad I heard from them before I go—I know they would come if they could." We shall leave here at 3:35 tomorrow. Eddie and Anna will come with me.

Mary requests that the funeral services take place in the church—she had no choice of preacher. I think however owing to the warm weather and the long time between her death and our arrival there that it may be better to have the service at the cemetary only.

I will telegraph you Monday morning of the progress we are making so that you will know if all is moving along all right or not.

Your son,
A.C. Titus

There were no other letters in the group about the incident. But I can't help wondering what happened to Titus and his two children. Did they return to Kansas? Did the father remarry? Did the family remain together? There may be children or grandchildren of Eddie Titus or his sister Anna living somewhere in the United States today. Nothing would make me happier than to turn these two letters over to their descendents and share those pieces of family history with them.

This is an example of the importance of content.

If, for the same cost, you could buy either a document signed by Buffalo Bill Cody or a letter written by him, which would you choose? A signed letter is usually more valuable than a signed document, not only because it shows more of the person's handwriting but because of its potential content. If Cody wrote a simple thank you note to a friend, the autographic value would outweigh the content value. But a personal letter to Mrs. Cody explaining financial struggles with the Wild West Show would easily surpass autographic value alone.

Content may also reveal "historical association." I recently bought a collection of stock certificates that included an Arizona Territory mining stock issued to Ed Schiefflin. Collectors familiar with Arizona history—Tombstone, to be exact—might recognize Schiefflin as a key figure in the Tombstone mining district that eventually extracted $40 million in silver from the desert ground.

The stock is not signed by Schiefflin so there is no autographic value; however, its content connects Schiefflin's discovery with the founding of one of the West's most notorious

PAT H. HAYES, UNDERSHERIFF　　　　　　　　　　　　　　　　ORREN BABBITT, DEPUTY SHERIFF

FRANK B. ROACH, SHERIFF
LARAMIE COUNTY, WYOMING

CHEYENNE, April 17 1916

Dear Brother Harry.

(Boy) born April 14th 1916

Allie and the little fellow getting along "fine" now. I think Allie may be able to come home next Sunday if she has good luck. they are at the Hospital now. I sure have all the work I can do and I was out of town so much that it got on my nerves. I tried to get home every night & had to do some fancy driving to do it. I drove from Chugwater here in 2 hours & 30 minutes. and one afternoon I drove 72 miles in 2 hours & 45 minutes. I was out chaseing the man who held up the Union Pacific train for three days & then got Lon to take the trail where I left off and he is still out. I just had to come back. they offer $5.500.00 for him. I know who he is & have a good discription of him. I sure hope we may get him.

Love to all
Frank

Wyoming Sheriff Frank Roach died less than a week after writing this 1916 letter to his brother announcing the birth of his son. In the letter Roach told his brother of trying to capture a train robber: "I was out chasing the man who held up the Union Pacific train for three days and then got Lon to take the trail where I left off and he is still out...." A few days later Roach was killed along the Wyoming-Colorado border while chasing the robbers.

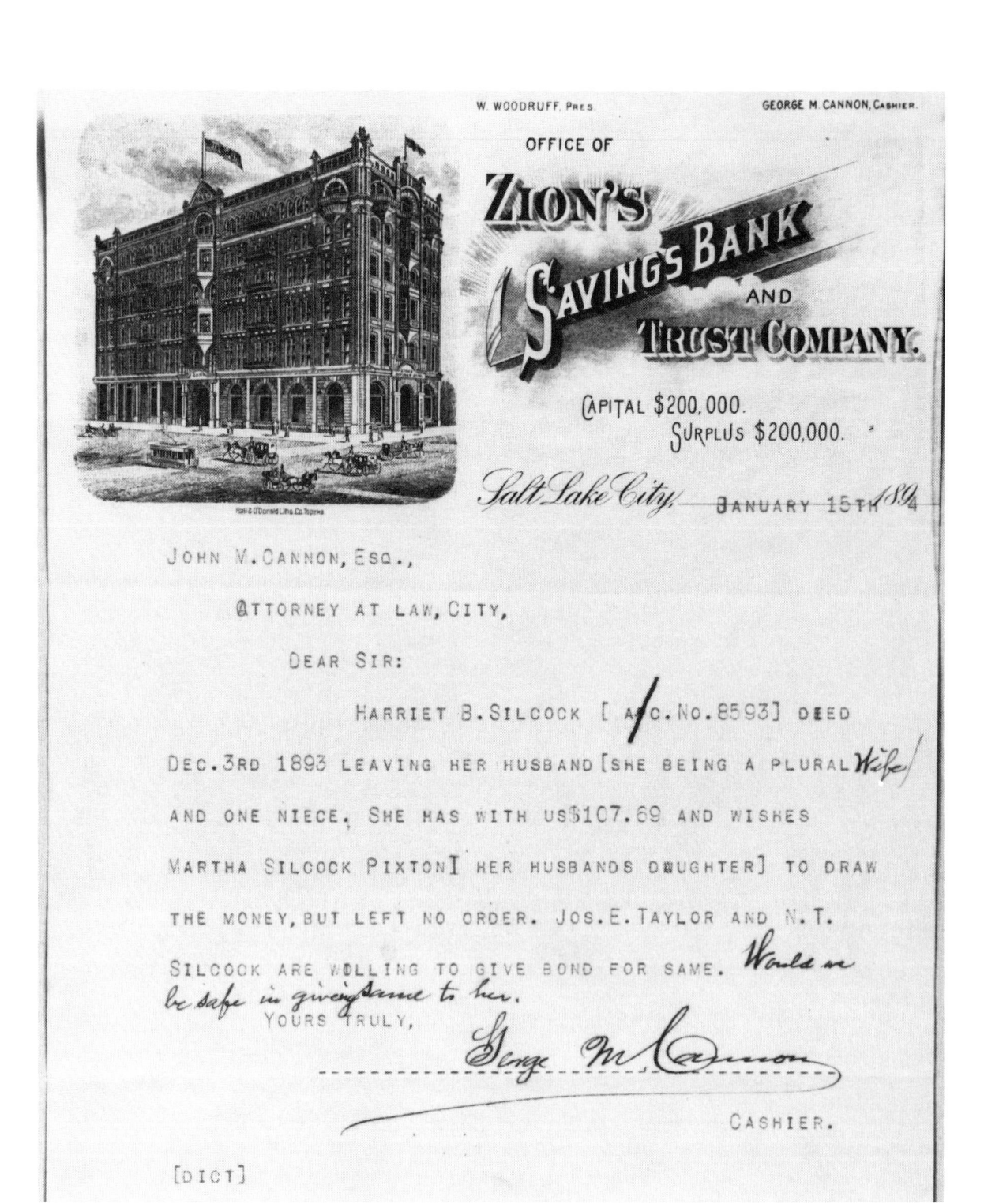

```
                              W. WOODRUFF, PRES.        GEORGE M. CANNON, CASHIER.
                                    OFFICE OF
                              ZION'S SAVINGS BANK
                                        AND
                                   TRUST COMPANY.
                                 CAPITAL $200,000.
                                  SURPLUS $200,000.

                        Salt Lake City, JANUARY 15TH 1894

JOHN M. CANNON, ESQ.,

    ATTORNEY AT LAW, CITY,

    DEAR SIR:

        HARRIET B. SILCOCK [A/C. NO. 8593] DIED

DEC. 3RD 1893 LEAVING HER HUSBAND [SHE BEING A PLURAL Wife]

AND ONE NIECE. SHE HAS WITH US $107.69 AND WISHES

MARTHA SILCOCK PIXTON [ HER HUSBANDS DAUGHTER] TO DRAW

THE MONEY, BUT LEFT NO ORDER. JOS. E. TAYLOR AND N. T.

SILCOCK ARE WILLING TO GIVE BOND FOR SAME. Would we
be safe in giving same to her.
        YOURS TRULY,
                                George M Cannon
                                              CASHIER.

[DICT]
```

When Brigham Young formed Zion's Bank in 1873, there was little more than the faith in the Mormon Church behind it. As this 1894 letter shows, the bank's capital had increased to $200,000, and Wilford Woodruff served as president of both the Mormon Church and Zion's Bank. The letter refers to the recent death of a woman who was a "plural [polygamous] wife."

mining towns. Although the content is not as compelling as it might be in a letter, the document is important by way of historical association.

Sometimes content can be difficult to decipher, presenting you with an opportunity to piece together clues and information. Dealers may sell letters or other documents with potentially valuable content inexpensively because they have not taken the time to examine them carefully. Perhaps the person's penmanship makes the content difficult to read. Only through collecting and handling old documents will you slowly but surely get better at interpreting various styles of writing.

A letter with good content might describe an encounter with Indians, or maybe describe a shoot-out or hanging, or it may tell of traveling by stagecoach or working in a mine. Any words that provide us a glimpse into someone's thoughts or experiences from the Old West can be fascinating. The more vivid and detailed the content, the better.

Some people coped with the hardships of frontier living by keeping a sense of humor about them, as the content of a miner's letter in my collection suggests. A young miner in Holland, Oregon, wrote an amusing and saucy letter to his brother in 1903 while passing the time away:

Dear Ike,

Was terribly surprised to hear from you. Letters just feel like a "set-em-up" up here in the wilds. This is a good place for an old eternal grouch like me though. We are forty miles from anywhere—the nearest piece of civilization is a post office and blacksmith shop about one mile below us.

My panama, that dear panama you so kindly relieved me of on the day I left—I might just as well have left your hat. Haven't worn it since I left Poly Alto. Overalls, flannel shirt, high boots and a slouch hat make up my wardrobe. Might just as well wear a fig leaf and a smile, the fig leaf would be superfluous for it would make a covering for wood ticks and ants—"P"-ants, not the kind you think I mean.

Can't fool me we don't have them. Let me contradict myself. My aunt is the old sow, my Uncle Old Jim the horse and my wife—well she filled up on dutch cheese and passed a whey.

Ike, I'm sort of worried for you said nothing of "our girls" across the way. I'm longing with all my heart to hear just a word from them. Can't you satisfy that long feeling of mine and offer the words that will once more unite me with Mother Earth and God's own country—the Palo Alto Farm. Don't be light, Ike, give me a line the first opportunity that offers and you will make me feel more like living.

Yours,
Wm. K. Roosevelt

Office of the Kenyon Mining Company

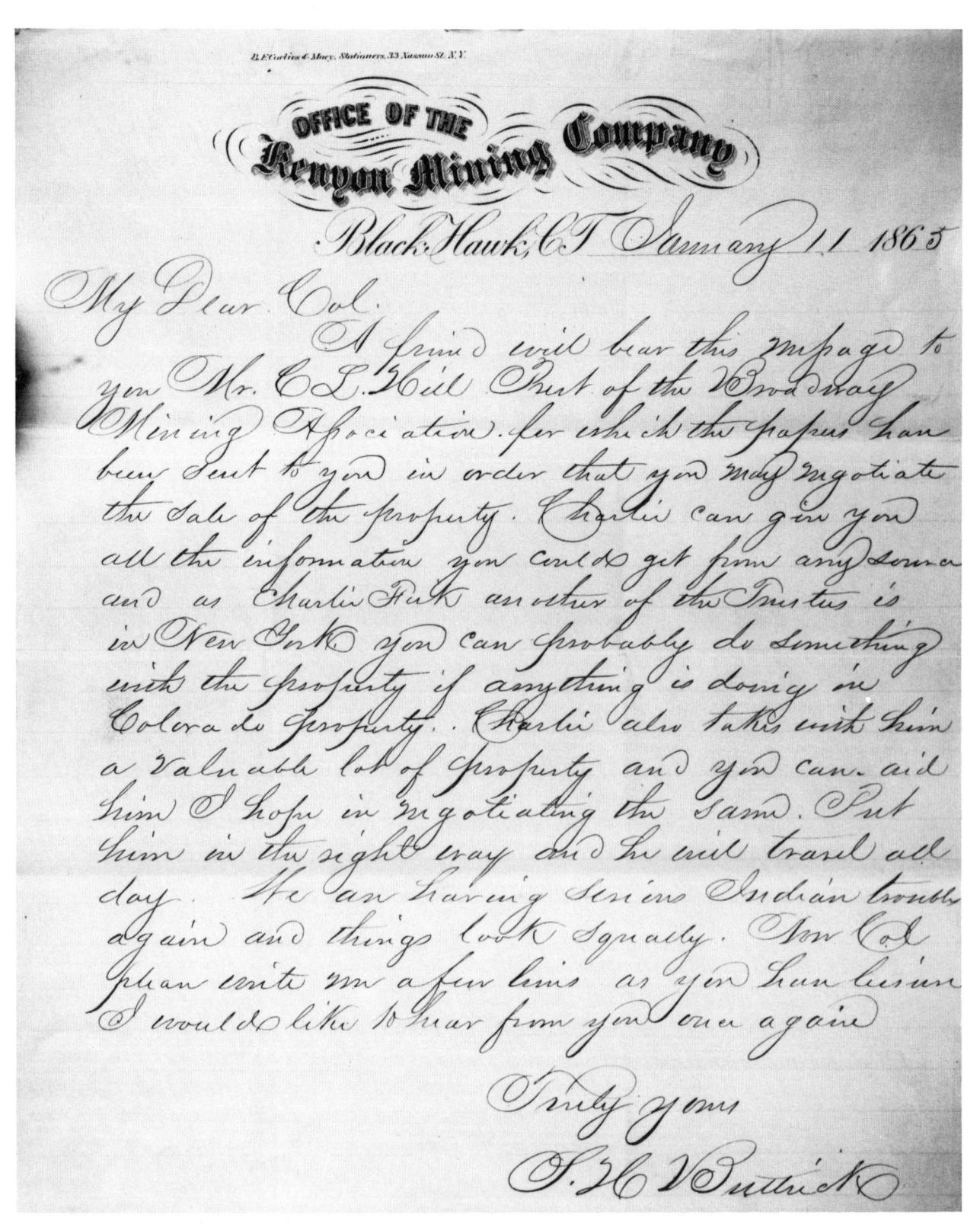

Black Hawk, C.T. January 11 1865

My Dear Col.

A friend will bear this message to you Mr. C. L. Hill Trust of the Broadway Mining Association. for which the papers have been sent to you in order that you may negotiate the sale of the property. Charlie can give you all the information you could get from any source and as Charlie Fisk another of the Trustees is in New York you can probably do something with the property if anything is doing in Colorado Property. Charlie also takes with him a valuable lot of property and you can aid him I hope in negotiating the same. Put him in the right way and he will travel all day. We are having serious Indian trouble again and things look squally. Now Col. please write me a few lines as you have leisure I would like to hear from you once again

Truly yours

S. H. V. Buttrick

This 1865 correspondence on letterhead from a Colorado Territory mining camp details working conditions at the mines and ongoing mining activities. The writer closed his letter by saying, "We are having serious Indian trouble again and things look squally..."

In one of our 1988 auctions we sold an excellent four-page letter dated 1903 from a father in Nome, Alaska Territory, to his son. In it he described the harsh winter conditions and his day-long attempt to help a freighter who had abandoned his wagon and horses a few miles from town during a snowstorm the day before. His graphic, eyewitness account of the life-and-death struggle of the half-frozen horses and their attempts to save them was fascinating and revealing.

The pre-auction estimate on the letter's value was $100. It sold for over $250 with commission. The proud owner understood the importance of the content and bid in relation to what he felt it was worth.

Letters aren't the only documents where content counts. Some documents are valuable for their subject matter. I own a colorful warrant, for instance, from Montana Territory dated March 31, 1884, paying a true mountain man $365 as "Bounty for killing 14 Bears, 14 Mountain Lions, 84 Wolves and 115 Coyotes." The territory had an eradication program against these and other animals during this period and paid set amounts for the skins of various animals. I can picture that old trapper in my mind—through the long, cold winter in the wilds of Montana he'd return to his crude cabin in the evening after spending long, ardous hours hunting and tracking down these wily and dangerous animals.

To assure success in the growth and colonization of Montana for both settlers and ranchers, the territory placed a bounty on certain predators. This 1884 territorial warrant authorized the treasury to pay $365 to R. A. Richie as "bounty for killing 14 bears, 14 mountain lions, 84 wolves, and 115 coyotes."

Another warrant in my collection was issued to an Indian named Fire Crow, paying him bounty for killing "One Bear and one Mountain Lion." Fire Crow endorsed the warrant on its verso with an "X." Surely he used a rifle to bring down his prey. Or did he?

Content in early western documents, then, may include information gleaned from letters or other narrative accounts as well as any from of historical association or unusual subject matter. Sometimes the document will be sold on these points and will be priced accordingly. With patience and diligence, though, you'll occasionally find important or interesting documents with unusual content at a fraction of their real collector value. Accurately interpreting the content of a document may increase its value significantly.

CHAPTER FIVE
Fakes, Forgeries and Theft

Each collecting field—whether fine art, numismatics (coin collecting), vases, or autographs—has its known counterfeits and reproductions. In the field of western historical documents there are some known forgeries and fakes, but they are relatively few. Of larger concern is the growing incident of document theft from institutions.

Western document forgery usually involves modern ink applied to old blank documents to make them appear as though they had been issued. The most widely publicized forgeries to date are the autographed western rarities penned by master forger Mark Hofmann in Utah. More on that later.

If there is one single fake document that has most fooled the general public during recent decades, I'd say it is the $1,000 promissory note, issue #8894, dated December 15, 1840, from the Bank of the United States. The attractive 4"x8" financial document features six vignettes of national figures including Benjamin Franklin and Alexander Hamilton. It started showing up as a novelty item at carnivals and county fairs around the country in the 1960s. It looks authentic enough—its paper is brown and somewhat wrinkled, as though it had aged naturally for many years. But the date and issue number of this fake note are now well known among collectors.

Several times a year I get inquiries from people who want to know something about promissory note #8894. The stories about how the notes turn up are usually pretty interesting in themselves. One woman told me she found the note in her great-grandmother's Bible. Another party told me their note was in an old trunk they bought at an auction. They said the trunk had been locked up so long that they needed a locksmith to open it. I smiled to myself and informed the new owners their trunk couldn't have been locked up too long, since the 1840 promissory note inside was actually printed no more than twenty or thirty years ago! Fakes have no real collector value. A forgery, however, is another thing.

Since forming America West Archives in 1979, I have received dozens of inquires from people asking the value of this note. Despite its aged appearance, it is not authentic and has no collector value. This note, bearing the 1841 date and serial number 8894, was mass-produced several decades ago and sold as a novelty item. This particular version has the word "COPY" printed in its bottom corner, but others I have seen do not.

Fakes

A few years ago I attended a gun show in Salt Lake City. It was a major event with hundreds of tables, several of which displayed old documents and paper Americana. A "dealer" from Texas at one table offered a group of western relics and ephemera, including a cabinet-card photograph signed by sharpshooter Annie Oakley. The amazing thing about this autographed photo was the price: $150. The genuine article would more likely cost about $1,500.

The dealer assured me it was an Annie Oakley autograph, and certainly it was a photograph of her. But the more I studied the autograph, the more suspicious I became. The signature at the bottom of the cabinet card was in pencil—a sharp-pointed one at that. The penmanship looked unusually modern for a woman who had died in 1926.

I told the dealer I would buy the photograph if he would keep it until he returned to Texas and then send me a photocopy of the picture so I could compare the autograph to an authentic Annie Oakley signature in one of my reference books. The dealer promised to do so, but I never heard from him again. I even wrote him several weeks later asking for the photocopy but received no response. His silence assures me that he knew the piece was a forgery.

Another incident involves a letter I recently received from a man in Omaha, Nebraska, offering to sell me an autograph of Sitting Bull. The original signature was on a 2"x3" piece of paper, which I was told had been in the family ever since the man's great-grandmother obtained it when she met Sitting Bull on a railroad excursion. The seller also sent me a copy of a ten-year old letter he'd sent to an autograph collector with the collector's reply and offer for it.

The photocopy of the signature compared well with my sources, so I made an offer to buy it based on the condition that I could examine the original. The seller sent it to me and I was immediately disappointed. Rather than an authentic ink signature, this appeared to have been printed or possibly stamped in light purple.

I tracked down the collector who the seller had contacted ten years earlier and learned that he, too, had been suspicious of the signature and had forwarded copies of it to several dealers, who also doubted its authenticity. Despite him telling the seller that the signature was not authentic, here was the man ten years later trying to peddle it to me with the "grandma-on-the-train" story. I returned the "original" signature to him in a 29-cent envelope and told him it was worthless.

COLLECTORS BEWARE! That fake Sitting Bull signature may still be on the warpath somewhere on the collector's market.

A few unintentionally forged documents are known to exist. One group that immediately comes to mind are the legal documents of Lincoln County, New Mexico Territory, signed by Sheriff Pat Garrett, who permitted his deputies to fill out his paperwork. I have seen three different examples of Garrett's signature on arrest warrants and complaints: some are signed "Pat Garrett, Sheriff, by John Doe, Deputy"; others are signed by deputies as "Pat Garrett, Sheriff," without the deputy's signature, giving the appearance of an authentic signature; still others are those authentically signed by Pat Garrett. Of course, you want to avoid buying a document signed by one of Garrett's deputies but sold an authentic Garrett autograph. In at least two instances I'm aware of this happening, and both documents came from autograph dealers who simply hadn't done their homework.

Autographs of some famous westerners are hard to find in standard autograph reference works, and if you do find one, it's usually just a single signature to use for reference purposes. This is inadequate as a safeguard against being duped. It's one of those unspoken lessons you learn from dealing in the markets.

Most dealers guarantee the authenticity of the autographs they sell, which protects you as a collector from fraud. If the autograph is later proven not to be authentic, the dealer will refund your money. Avoid buying autographs from dealers who do not guarantee authenticity.

Printed reproductions, or "commemoratives," also pose problems in the marketplace. I have been contacted on numerous occasions by people wanting to know the value of papers that turned out to be modern reprints of originals. Governments and organizations commonly produce copies of an original document to commemorate an anniversary or other special occasion.

There are a number of reprinted documents concerning Abraham Lincoln on the collector's market. A few years ago I received a letter from a party who offered an "original" broadside announcing the president's attendance at Ford's Theatre, where, of course, Lincoln was assassinated. Had the broadside been authentic, it would be rare and valuable. But a Lincoln memorabilia expert I checked with told me the broadside was only 50-75 years old and had been reproduced and sold as a souvenir.

I have also seen reprinted copies of the *New York Herald* announcing Lincoln's assassination. But the *Herald* never had an "8:10 A.M. Edition," as this paper professed to be. An original issue would cost hundreds; the recent-vintage reprint has no real collector value.

Watch carefully for commemorative documents because they can be deceiving. They are usually printed on old presses using a special paper that makes them look authentic. And some of them, such as some important historical documents from Virginia I examined a while back, are very good imitations. These documents were in too clean of a condition to be two hundred years old, yet I can see how someone with less experience might be fooled by them.

There is still plenty of Confederate "funny money" on the collector's market, and it can fool anyone who doesn't have authentic examples of Civil War currency to compare it to. Be wary of money, old newspapers with important headlines, or seemingly old documents with historic content or signatures, especially if their condition is noticeably clean. I have seen such items sold by dealers and in auctions as authentic—unintentionally, of course, which only proves that even dealers and auctioneers can be fooled now and then.

Forgery

Examples of forged historical western documents are few and far between. The problem is not very widespread primarily because it's difficult to manage all the elements with older documents; however, forgery is a growing problem in modern autographs, even if you discount the confusion caused by automatic signature devices (autopens) and rubber stamps. The autographs of Marilyn Monroe and Elvis Presley, for example, are two of the most commonly forged signatures on the autograph market today.

Obtaining the proper ink and paper to forge an old document is difficult in itself, but the usual giveaway in spotting a forgery lies with the forger's pen or penmanship. Modern handwriting is unlike the prevalent styles of a hundred years ago. And the older style is difficult to imitate.

In several instances over the years, I've found unissued documents that were filled in by hand at a later date in an attempt to make the document look like it had been issued and, therefore, more valuable. One collection I bought included a 1902 California mining stock that had been filled in with a ball-point pen. Since the ball-point wasn't invented until the 1940s, it obviously couldn't have been used in 1902!

A few years ago a colleague sent me photocopy of a document signed by Bat Masterson as sheriff of Ford County, Kansas, to see if I wanted to include it in an auction. Most common legal documents, including complaints and warrants, were filled out by a deputy or undersheriff. Even when the sheriff was supposed to sign such documents, usually the deputy who handled the paperwork signed for him. And this happened on the Masterson document; the deputy had filled it out and signed it on the verso. Above the deputy's signature, in ink, was Bat Masterson's signature—in pencil and squeezed inbetween a line of writing and the deputy's signature.

After the Annie Oakley incident I learned to closely examine western autographs signed in pencil, although they were used a hundred years ago just as they are today. I couldn't say for sure that Masterson's signature was a forgery, but it

—46—

This 1902 stock certificate reveals a major sign of forgery. Can you spot the problem? It has been filled out and signed with a ball-point pen—a product invented during the 1940s. Someone has filled in this unissued certificate in an attempt to make it look issued and thus worth more to a collector. The embossed seal is also missing from the bottom left corner.

looked suspicious enough that I declined to include the document in our auction.

Later research revealed to me that on the month and year Masterson was to have signed the document, he had been tracking a horse thief in a neighboring state. I don't know how long he was gone, but I do know that of all the other western law enforcement documents I have handled, the signatures have always appeared in ink.

Virtually all early western documents were written in ink. Blunt pencils were commonly used in the latter 1800s, especially in regions where cold weather might have prevented the ink from flowing as it should. But documents of a more permanent nature almost always were written in ink. In a winter letter Robert LeRoy Parker (Butch Cassidy) wrote to his brother from Wyoming, he apologized for writing in pencil because the ink had froze. Soldiers during the Civil War and on the western frontier commonly wrote letters in pencil since it was not practical to carry ink in the field.

The Hofmann Incident. Perhaps the most notorious case of document forgery and murder in the twentieth century occurred in Utah in 1987. Suddenly the national media spotlight focused on the secretive world of rare documents and high finances. Before that light dimmed, Mark Hofmann was convicted of two bombing murders, fraud, and theft by deception.

Hofmann, a rare documents collector/dealer specializing in early Mormon material, appeared from obscurity around 1980. He continually surprised Mormon Church historians and rare manuscript collectors with his discoveries of important documents, some which contradicted church history and challenged Mormon doctrine. Within a few years his amazing discoveries penetrated other collecting realms, including western autographs.

In 1985 Hofmann quietly peddled a number of promissory notes for $5,000-$10,000 on the collector's market. The notes bore the illiterate "X" signature of mountain man Jim Bridger and came from Fort Bridger, Utah Territory. Hofmann also sold various early Mormon documents to the Mormon Church and unsuspecting dealers, collectors, and auction houses around the country. I have three books in my reference library that show some of the spurious documents that came from Hofmann; since these were printed before his arrest and exposure as a forger, however, all of the forgeries are listed as authentic.

Hofmann's forgeries escaped detection for some time, in part because he used genuine old paper and developed a specific type of ink from an 1800s formula. He also traded and sold authentic old documents to help cover his forgery sales. Several of his forgeries had been declared "authentic" by two well-known autograph dealers, proving the fallability of authentification. Even the Federal Bureau of Investigation had been duped when it originally declared Hofmann's famous "Salamander" letter authentic.

Hofmann's undoing literally exploded when he was connected with the bombing deaths of two people in an attempt to divert attention from his financial debts, botched document deals, and fraudulant dealings.

George Throckmorton and William Flynn, both members of the Southwestern Association of Forensic Document Examiners, spent eighteen months examining nearly 450 documents sold or traded by Hofmann along with others taken from his home after his arrest. They conducted a battery of special tests, including ultraviolet and infrared light examinations, microscopic examination, paper and ink tests, and searches for anomalies (artificial aging) and anachronisms (the improper use of wording for the time period).

Throckmorton and Flynn found 107 forgeries and 68 questionable documents. The weak link in Hofmann's scheme turned out to be his special ink. He used a formula from autograph dealer Charles Hamilton's book, *Great Forgers and Famous Fakes*, which police found in Hofmann's home after his arrest. The ink bled and ran in an uncommon manner, leaving an unusual cracking pattern visible only under a microscope.

Most people associate Hofmann's forgeries with Mormon documents, which indeed received most of the publicity. But subsequent investigations have shown that he forged many signatures, including those of Daniel Boone, Napoleon Bonaparte, William Bonney (Billy the Kid), Davy Crockett, Charles Dickens, Button Gwinett, Nathan Hale, Francis Scott Key, Jack London, Abraham Lincoln, Herman Melville, William Quantrill, Paul Revere, Porter Rockwell, Betsy Ross, Joseph Smith, Myles Standish, Mark Twain, and Brigham Young. Hofmann may also have forged the signatures of Wild Bill Hickok and Wyatt Earp. When police searched his home they found a signed photograph of Butch Cassidy crumpled up in his trash can—a rejected forgery.

Hofmann went to prison for his crimes. Although the controversy over the content of his Mormon forgeries quickly died out, it continues still over who owns his forgeries today.

In 1989 a former bookstore owner admitted to forging a number of rare printed broadsides and imprints pertaining to early Texas history. Produced in the early 1970s and acquired by other Texas dealers when the bookstore closed in 1972, fifteen of the forgeries came to light only after someone realized that twenty copies of the famous 1836 broadside of the Texas Declaration of Independence existed in 1987, while only five had been known to exist prior to 1970. Some fifty other forgeries housed in universities, libraries, and among private collectors were confirmed by a master printer after the type faces used to print some of the documents were found to be of 1900 vintage instead of pre-1850.

Serious forgers seem to go for the big money, manufacturing the rarest documents instead of reproducing those valued at less than $1,000. Thus, the problem exists more in the upper echelons of rare documents and autographs than in the general marketplace. Although a few forgeries of rare, expensive western documents are known to exist, it's safe to assume that about 99 percent are authentic.

Again, forgeries of early western documents are rare. You need not be overly concerned with the possibility of encountering a forged document. However, an area that should concern you is being offered rare and historical documents that have been stolen.

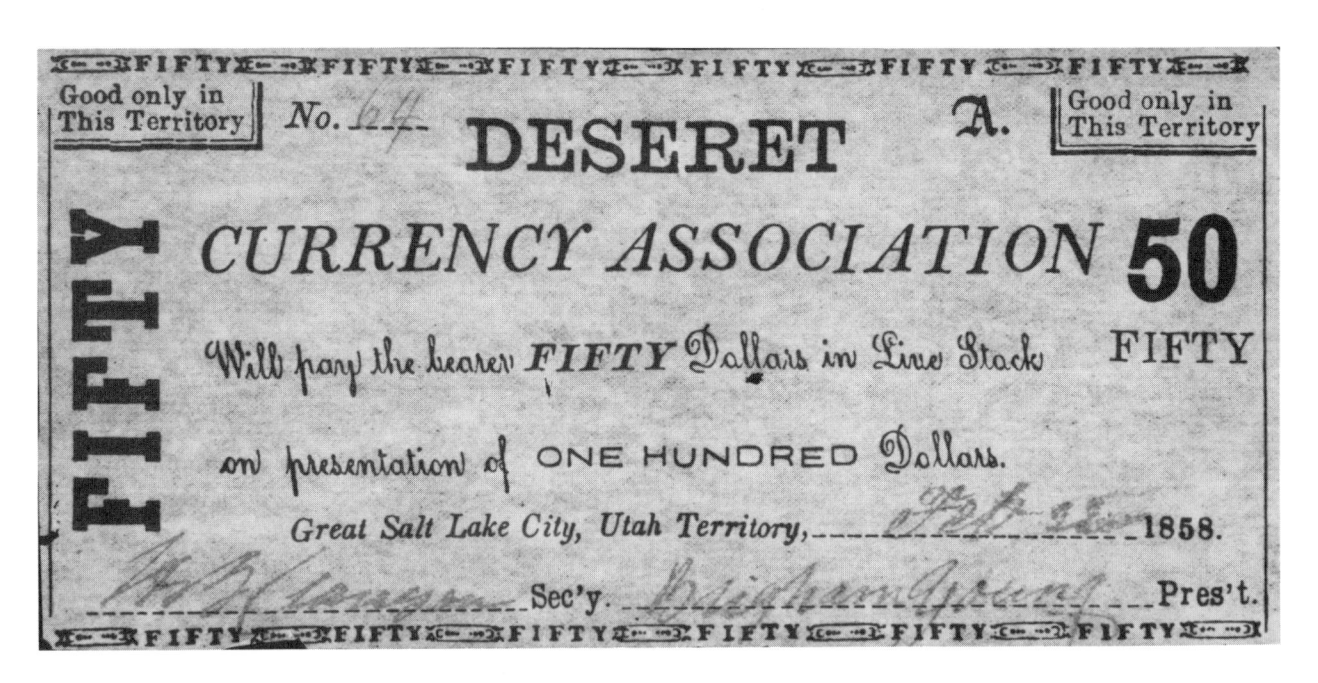

In 1858 the Mormon Church formed the Deseret Currency Association to establish a means of currency in their cash-starved territory. The unique scrip was backed by livestock. Unfortunately, the two notes shown here were manufactured by forger Mark Hofmann, who printed the notes and forged the signatures of Brigham Young and Hiram Clawson, then sold them as authentic.

Many early Utah Territory communities established by Mormon settlers organized cooperative stores as a means of exchanging goods in lieu of scarce currency. The stores issued scrip notes redeemable in hard goods for services rendered. About 200 early Utah communities had cooperatives that flourished between 1868 and 1884. This 25-cent scrip note for the Spanish Fork Co-operative Institution is a forgery signed by Mark Hofmann.

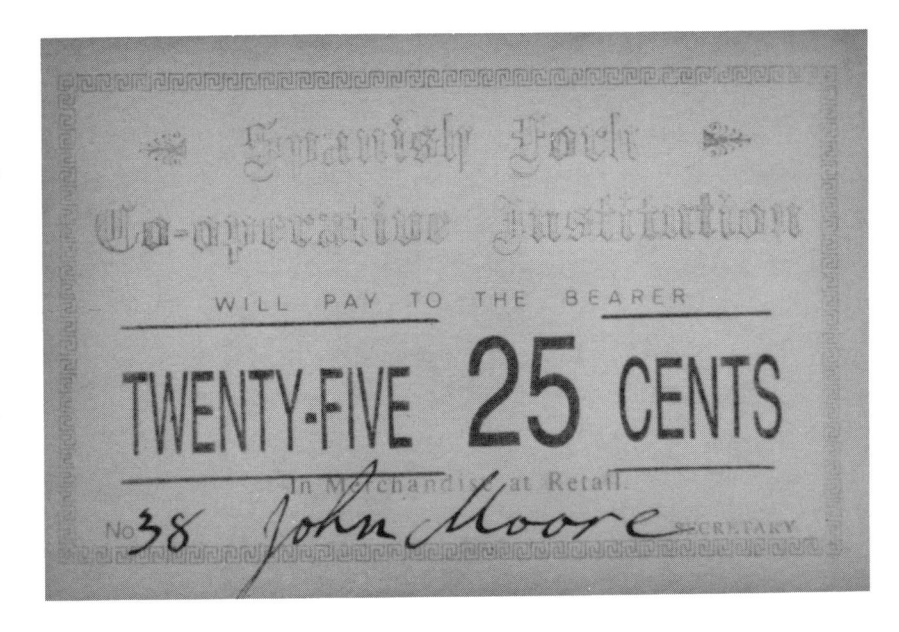

While music played an important role in early Mormon history, the Nauvoo Music Association was created by forger Mark Hofmann. He manufactured two types of stock, then forged the signatures on them using two different pens.

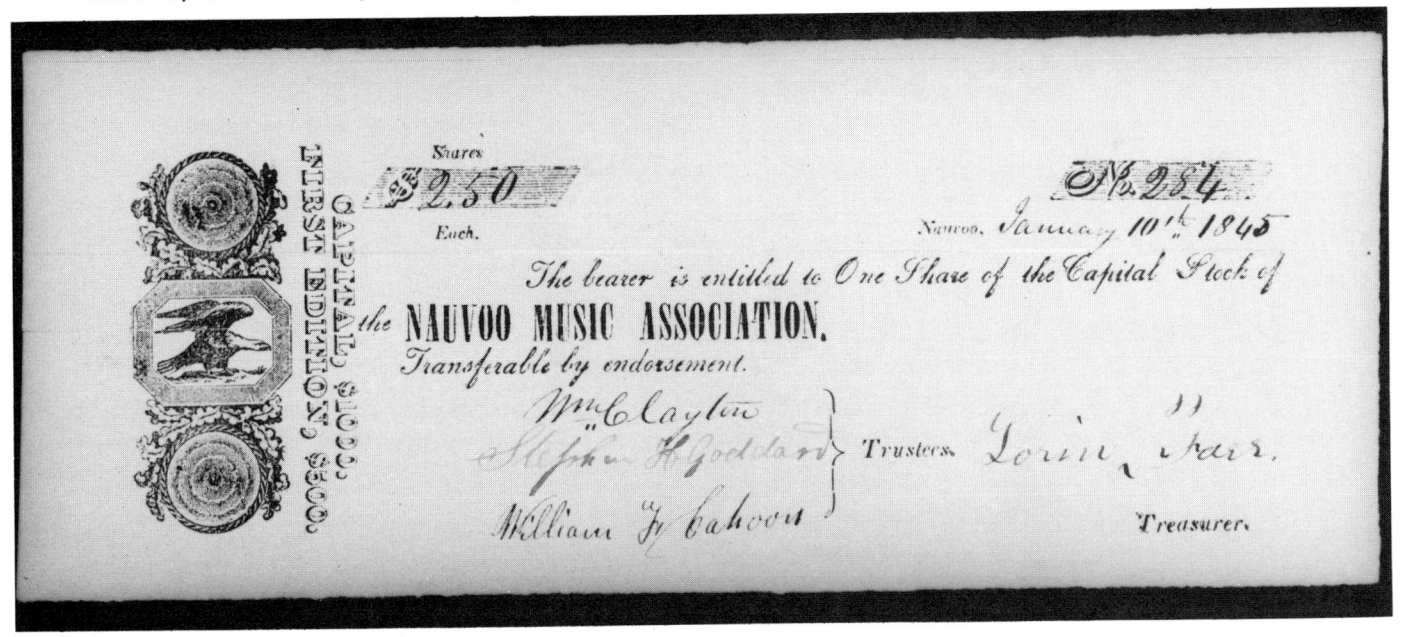

Theft

Stolen historical documents is a growing problem. As documents become rarer and more valuable, the lure of making a large, quick profit, especially to those who have access to institutional collections, has become more enticing.

The Gun Dealer. A few years ago I was contacted by a man who had an attractive framed photograph and note handwritten by Bat Masterson. I offered to help find a buyer by brokering it and sent out inquiries to some potentially interested parties. Luckily, one of the people I contacted recognized the Masterson piece as one from a sour deal ten years earlier involving stolen documents; that person alerted the original owner, who in turn contacted me.

The owner had traded the Masterson piece in 1980 for other western lawmen documents from a gun dealer, then resold the documents he had obtained in the trade. Soon after, he was contacted by the F.B.I. and informed that the items he had traded his Masterson piece for were stolen from the Dodge City, Kansas Courthouse. He was instructed to buy back the stolen documents and return them to the Dodge City Courthouse. In court the gun dealer admitted his role in the crime. The gun dealer was supposed to return the Bat Masterson piece to its owner, but the man never received it. Meanwhile, the gun dealer had disappeared, apparently taking the Bat Masterson piece with him. It was about ten years later when I entered the picture.

The gun dealer had changed his name by the time he offered the Masterson piece to me. It's much harder, though, to change one's handwriting style. So I checked his handwriting against a sample held by the the real owner of the Masterson piece in an attempt to verify whether this man was the gun dealer who had disappeared with the piece years earlier. His last name had a 't' in it, just as the gun dealer's last name had, and after studying the signatures of both names I discovered two things: 1) the handwriting style was identical, and 2) the man had a peculiar way of crossing his 't.' I shared my findings with the real owner of the Bat Masterson piece, who contacted the authorities and was later happily reunited with the autographed photo.

The Bibliomaniac. In 1990 the F.B.I. uncovered what has since been called the largest theft of rare books and documents of the twentieth century. Stephen Blumberg of Ottumwa, Iowa, allegedly had been stealing books and manuscripts from nearly 300 university libraries, museums, and other institutions for over fifteen years. Several times he had been caught, but nobody realized the severity of his thefts until federal investigators converged upon his quiet home. Inside, they found an estimated $20 million in rare books and manuscripts. The stolen goods weighed nineteen tons and required seven trips using a large moving van to remove all of the material. Every room in the house was literally stacked with books and folders from the floor to the ceiling.

Blumberg apparently did not steal the material for resale or profit. He simply loved books. Normally such a person would be called a bibliophile, but one Iowa newspaper classified Blumberg as a "bibliomanic." Some of the materials came from such prestigious university libraries as Harvard, Norte Dame, and UCLA.

The Stratton Stocks. Another case of possible theft involved signed stock certificates from Colorado's Gold Crater Mining Company. Suddenly appearing at auctions around 1988, these certificates bore the signature of Cripple Creek mining millionaire Winfield Stratton. Prior to that time, collectors of obsolete stocks and bonds had never seen Stratton's autograph on the market. All of Winfield Stratton's personal and business papers had been stored in a vault in the Myron Stratton home (named after his father) in Colorado Springs since his death in 1902. Stratton had willed most of his wealth to the building of the Myron Stratton home as a place for the homeless and destitute.

The source of the signed stock certificates was a part-time writer/collector from Colorado. In 1986, while working on a book about Cripple Creek that included a chapter on Winfield Stratton, he approached the repository of Stratton's papers, Myron Stratton Home, and requested information for his book. The administrators told him that Stratton's personal and business papers had never been inventoried, so the writer offered to undertake the task. Ironically, about a year later, he began selling Gold Crater Mining certificates signed by Winfield Stratton. He even offered some to me, claiming he acquired them from the East Coast, but I declined to buy them.

Whether the Stratton-signed stocks actually came from the Myron Stratton Home remains a mystery, since no prior inventory of its holdings existed before the writer offered to conduct one. But what is known is that the man started selling the Stratton-signed stocks soon after he inventoried the collection, and, until that time, I have not been able to verify that Winfield Stratton's autograph had never been offered for sale.

Such episodes of possible theft can prove embarrassing to the officials responsible for safeguarding historical papers; the incidents may reflect errors in their judgment or breaches in their security. Despite the unwanted publicity cases like this may spawn, recognizing the problem is an important step towards preventing it. Perhaps a reluctance to acknowledge the problem is how Blumberg got away with so many thefts.

The Casino Caper. One incident that did receive publicity in the fall of 1990 was the theft of ninety historical stock certificates valued at $35,000 from a Laughlin, Nevada, casino. A party in Arizona contacted me and offered to sell the stock certificates, including an original Standard Oil stock signed by John D. Rockefeller; other stocks bore the signatures of Henry Wells and James Fargo of Wells Fargo fame, explorer John C. Frémont, inventor Thomas Edison, former President Millard Fillmore, and Wall Street financiers Jay Gould and J. P. Morgan.

I asked the seller how he had acquired the stocks and was shocked to hear that he had found them in a trash dumpster. This made no sense to me, but the seller stood by his story; as if to make it more logical, he said several of the documents suffered water damaged since it was raining when he found them. He agreed to send me some photocopies.

A week later I still had not received the photocopies, so I called the seller. There were so many documents in the group that I asked if he'd mind bringing them to Cedar City instead of just sending copies. He explained that he had to go to California for a few days first and would contact me upon his return. Meanwhile, I began calling dealers to see if anyone knew about any missing or stolen collections that fit the description of the one being offered to me.

A scripophily dealer remembered selling a similiar collection six years earlier to an interior decorator for a casino in Laughlin, which framed the stocks and put them on display. It dawned on me then that the seller lived just across the Arizona border from the glittering lights of Laughlin's casinos—too close for comfort. The dealer offered to contact the purchaser and see if everything was in order, then get back to me.

Several days later the suspicious seller called and said he'd make the trip to Utah in another week. I began feeling caught between a rock and a hard place, so I decided to call the casino myself. After getting the run-around from one office to another, I eventually got through to the manager, who listened to my story and called me back the next day to verify that the casino's collection was indeed missing. It had been placed in storage during renovation, and my call had alerted them to the fact that it was missing.

By now I wished not to be involved. I encouraged the casino manager to take care of the matter and contact the seller directly before he could bring the stolen goods to Utah. I no longer wanted to see him or the certificates. But the manager called back and said law enforcement authorities wanted me to call the seller and set up a meeting in Laughlin where they could arrest the seller. I declined to get any further involved and just wanted out of the deal. The casino manager said he'd call me over the weekend after the seller was intercepted by the police.

The weekend came and went. The manager didn't call, but on Monday morning the seller did. He was in Cedar City with the certificates and wanted to meet me. Shocked and caught off guard, I told him to meet me in my office in an hour. Obviously the situation was too immediate for any help from Nevada and Arizona, so I called Cedar City Police Chief Pete Hansen and explained the problem to him.

Pete organized his men and the set-up, then played the role of an interested party who would help me buy the stolen stock certificates. The seller and his wife arrived, and we all discussed the certificates and the price. Then Pete and I asked for a chance to discuss the deal privately.

The couple left and planned to come back in a little while. When they got to the parking lot, police surrounded their car and arrested them, recovering the casino's property. A week before their July 1991 trial date and eight months after the arrest, the couple struck a plea bargain that spared them the consequences of a jury. Apparently they paid a stiff fine and the man served some jail time.

Theft of historical documents is a growing problem, and unsuspecting dealers and collectors can become victims. I encourage all who work with historical documents to minimize the incidents of thievery by reporting any suspicious offerings to the proper authorities.

Research Pays Off

Countless times over the past dozen years I have researched a signature or document and discovered important information that greatly increased its value. To the great advantage of collectors, many document dealers do not take the time to research the documents they sell. No doubt rare historical nuggets await discovery by you!

Anyone serious about investing time and money in a collection needs history and reference books to conduct research. Of course, if you live in an urban area, you no doubt have at least one library to turn to. But having a few dozen well-chosen books permits you to consult a good, basic reference library without leaving your house. My personal library consists of some 250 books along with complete sets of *True West, Old West*, and *Frontier Times* magazines. Of these, I find myself mostly using only a few dozen important sources. If you haven't already begun, now is the time to start building your own informal library of sources to assist your research.

Choosing books for your library is highly

subjective and depends quite a bit on your particular collecting field and interests. Keep your eyes and ears open when you discuss collecting with others. Subject guides and card catalogs at public or university libraries may also help your search for personal library books. One of my overall favorite books on the exploration, colonization, and development of the West is *Men to Match My Mountains* by Irving Stone. And a set I recommend merely for its breadth of coverage is the 26-volume Old West series from Time-Life Books. The books I list in the bibliography of this book may also be appropriate for many collectors.

You need not buy rare or out-of-print books to establish a well-rounded reference library. Shops that sell new and used books are good places to find what you're after. If you can't find a particular book, usually the store manager can order it for you. You can also buy books directly from the publisher. Many of the older western history classics are available as inexpensive reprints through various publishers. Most of the books in my library cost from $10 to $30. The information I've taken from them over the years has more than paid for the library.

If you collect western autographs, you'll probably want to own biographies (or autobiographies) of the key people in your collection as companion pieces to your signed documents. This is something I personally enjoy. For each autographed document in my collection, I have tried to find a book about the individual's life. I began collecting these books when I first started collecting documents. After acquiring a land grant signed by Texas Governor Sam Houston,

This mining stock, issued from South Dakota for the Diamondfield-Bullfrog district of southern Nevada and signed by gunslinger "Diamondfield" Jack Davis embodies the rags to riches story in the Old West. Hired as a "regulator" by cattle baron (and later Nevada Governor) John Sparks in the 1890s, Davis boasted of killing two sheepmen. He was arrested, convicted, and spent seven years in an Idaho jail. After his release he made a small fortune mining in southern Nevada and again served as a hired gunman during the mining labor strikes in 1907. The stock pictured is signed by Davis as president and was issued to Nevada mining and banking millionaire George Wingfield, who later hired Davis as his bodyguard during the labor strife.

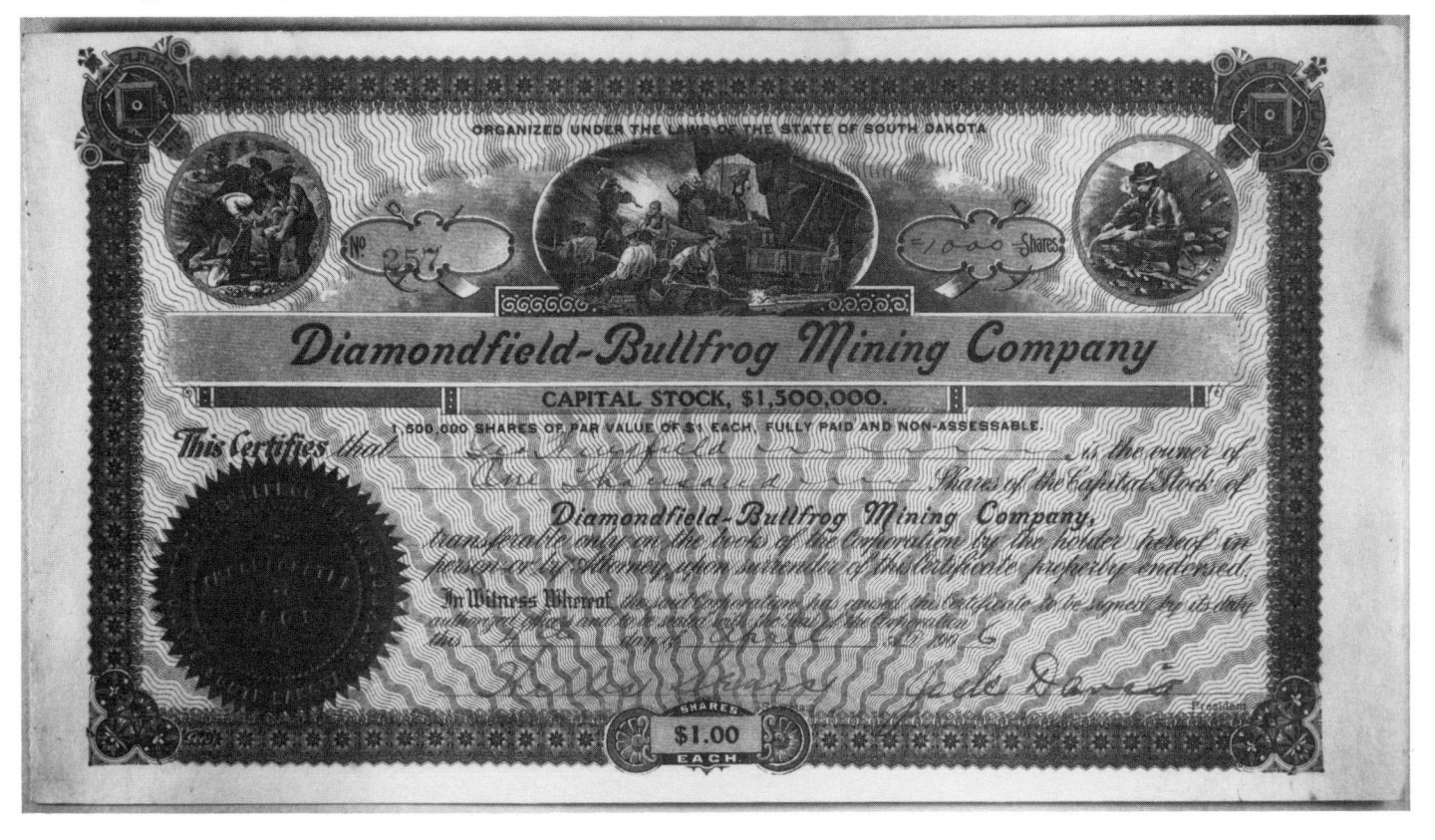

I found a biography of him detailing his fascinating career; it made the document all the more valuable and interesting to me, and now the practice has become an enjoyable habit.

I vividly remember the first autographed document I found by conducting my own research. I read the remarkable story of how a young, poor cowboy with a shady background and a fast six-shooter arrived in Tonopah, a small but booming Nevada mining camp, in the early 1900s. By simply pyramiding his winnings from an all-night card game at the Tonopah Club, this average cowpoke became a millionaire. By 1915 he owned every major bank in Nevada and held significant mining interests in Tonopah, Goldfield, and other mining camps. For two decades he wielded great influence with both political parties in the state. His name was George Wingfield. He lost his fortune as quickly as he made it when his banks were forced to close following the stock market crash of 1929.

The document I recognized as valuable was an early-1900s mining stock certificate signed by Wingfield. The first catalog I issued as a dealer offered a Wingfield-signed stock certificate for $16.50; with luck, a collector might find one today for $100. A stock certificate signed by him recently sold for $300 in a Beverly Hills autograph auction.

Another early, important document in my collection came from an East Coast mail auction. It was described simply as a signed 1859 indemnifying bond for freight suppied to Camp Floyd, Utah Territory. I won the bid, and when my newly purchased document arrived I saw that it had three signatures on it. One was "Wm. H. Russell." I thought the name sounded familiar but couldn't remember from where. A little research revealed that William Russell was one of the biggest freighters in the early West and founder/financier of the Pony Express. This knowledge instantly increased the document's value—as if by magic—twenty-fold. The consignor and auctioneer had not done their homework.

Dealers occasionally include historical information along with the important documents they sell. While this can be very helpful to you as a collector, remember that additional research on your part may go beyond whatever information the dealer (or seller) has put together. When you buy from a dealer who provides historical information with rare documents, you know you are dealing with someone who cares about history and who has taken the time to learn more about it.

All dealers should be knowledgeable about the material they sell. It's disappointing to run into those who can't answer questions a collector might ask before deciding to buy. They either haven't done their homework or aren't experts in their chosen field. A good dealer must be more than a great salesperson. Beware of overnight dealers who occasionally pop onto the market without any credentials or experience.

CHAPTER SIX

Assessing
Document Conditions, Cancellations
and Revenue Stamps

The amount of wear an old document shows affects its value. Although the condition of most old documents varies, collectors mostly desire those that are clean and as close as possible to their original condition. Knowing what defects you might encounter and understanding the varying degrees of condition should help you exercise good judgment in acquiring the best documents for your collection as well as taking care of them afterward.

Common defects on old documents include moisture stains, tears, glue or adhesive stains, taped repairs, moth or insect holes, acidic deterioration, sunlight spots, weak or broken fold lines, edge flaking or tearing, and cancellation marks. When spending your hard-earned money to build a quality collection, you must be aware of these conditions, what causes them, and how to spot and avoid those documents that show excessive wear.

A number of professional conservationists around the country can repair damaged documents. But the cost can be substantial, so always get an estimate first and make sure the document is worth repairing before agreeing to hire someone to do it. I once sent a photocopy of an autographed document with a six-inch tear to a conservator and found that the repair cost would exceed the value of the document. Since then I have avoided buying documents damaged to the point of needing such services. Of course, if the document is extremely rare and valuable, then professional restoration is worth considering.

In 1990 the Manuscript Society produced a fine booklet entitled *The Manuscript Society Criteria for Describing Manuscripts and Documents*. It sets guidelines for the condition and description of old papers and provides a format for objectively grading and describing documents in dealers' catalogs, which is better than the previous system where collectors and dealers used their own varied sets of criteria. The Manuscript Society sells its booklet to collectors and dealers.

Bear in mind that virtually all documents show some degree of wear, and this is certainly true of older papers. When you examine a document in person, always look over both its front and back carefully. Any time you buy, sell, or trade a document through the mail, always mention or ask about its defects; photocopies might not show tears and blemishes. Dealers usually will divulge defects in a document voluntarily, but careful collectors always purchase documents contingent upon a final, personal examination.

Most people know the experience of buying something, then later noticing defects they didn't realize existed when they bought the item. I have had my share of these, too, but I have become better at noticing things that might affect a document's value—usually tears or taped repairs. Most other defects are easier to spot. In the following paragraphs I will discuss various forms of damage and what might be done about them.

Fold tears. These are probably the most common defect on old documents. Some papers such as letters, stock certificates, insurance policies, and the like, were folded to fit into envelopes, folders, or safe deposit boxes. The folded areas get weak from folding and unfolding over the years, and sometimes tears develop along the fold lines. Fold tears usually do not detract from the value of a document unless they are numerous or lengthy. For preservation's sake, you should flatten folded documents and avoid refolding them.

Other tears. Tears not related to folds may be more detrimental to the document's value, as well as more difficult to repair. Some documents may have old cellophane or Scotch tape repairs made by well-intentioned but misguided parties. Older types of tape leave yellow stains behind; newer types probably won't yellow but may leave a sticky residue when removed. Generally, the longer the tear, the greater its affect on the document's value. Tears less than an inch or two in length can be repaired with professional archival repair tape. This is a special non-acidic, non-yellowing and nearly invisible tape. Never use any other type of tape to mend a torn document.

Moisture stains. You can spot water or damp stains by a characteristic rippling or slightly darkened appearance. Depending upon the document's paper type, the moisture that stained it can also contribute to its deterioration. This is especially true of the very early documents printed on thin paper. While certain tears can be repaired to halt further tearing, water damage cannot be corrected and must be accepted the way it is. A small water stain on an edge or in a corner shouldn't detract much from the document's value, but excessive or unsightly stains can make resale difficult.

Pests. Insects and rodents sometimes find old paper tasty. The damage they cause documents is detectible by the telltale evidence they leave behind. Insects bore small, pinhead-sized holes in paper, while mice chew larger, uneven holes. If the document is folded during this pest-fest, opening it reveals the multiple holes that result from several layers being eaten through at once. Fortunately, this problem is not very common.

Acid burns. You may occasionally find a document with ink burns caused by the acids in old ink. These usually appear only where the ink blobbed onto the paper or around signatures; eventually the ink may burn one or more small holes through the document. For documents printed on acidic paper, time is their worst enemy. The paper simply becomes fragile with age, especially along its edges where it becomes brown and deteriorates. In some cases, acidic paper can be treated with a high-tech spray that neutralizes the acid to prevent yellowing in old documents and extend their life; however, the spray may cause some inks to bleed, so the cure is not absolute.

The lack of timber and stones across the western plains with which to build fences, combined with increasingly frequent boundary conflicts between ranchers and farmers, was solved in the mid-1870s with the invention of barbed wire. The three million pounds of barbed wire manufactured in 1876 grew to eighty million pounds just four years later. This 1881 stock is from a company that produced the steel strands. Only 300 shares existed in this company, making this example a rarity.

This handwritten 1864 note from Fort Laramie (then within the boundaries of Idaho Territory) orders the post quartermaster to furnish a half bushel of corn to two men for their stock. The note explains, "Their horses have been stolen by the Indians and they have come about 65 miles to the fort for help." It is signed by William O. Collins, for whom Fort Collins was later named.

THE UNITED STATES,

To Wenap Snoot Dr.

DATE.		DOLLARS.	CTS.
1870 Sep. 30	For 3 Months Salary as Chief of the Umatilla Tribe of Indians Coms. July 1st and ending Sept. 30th 1870 at the rate of $500.00 per annum as per 5th Art Treaty June 9th 1855	125	00

Received at Umatilla Agency Or. Sept. 30th 1870, of Lieut W H Boyle U.S.A. U.S Ind Agent One Hundred and Twenty five Dollars, in full of the above account.

$125.00   Witness M Davenport   Wenap X Snoot (his mark)

(Signed in Quadruplicates.)

I Certify, on honor, that the above account is correct and just, and that I have actually, this 30th day of Sept. 1870, paid the amount thereof.

W H Boyle
1st Lt
U. S. Indian Agent.

To keep Indians in check, the military paid salaries to each Indian chief for governing the members of his tribe. This 1870 military voucher from the Umatilla Indian Agency in Oregon shows that Chief "Wenap Snoot," signing with an "X," received $125 for three-months' salary. It is also signed by noted Indian fighter Lt. William Boyle, who has signed as the U.S. Indian Agent.

James Butler "Wild Bill" Hickok wrote this letter from Monticello, Kansas Territory, where he served as a constable when he was twenty-one years old. In the opening lines, he wrote that he "served three summons this morning. There has been 25 horses stolen here within the last ten days...." Hickok was murdered while playing poker in a saloon at Deadwood, South Dakota, in 1876. He was holding a pair of aces and eights, now immortalized as the "dead man's hand."

VAL VERDE COUNTY

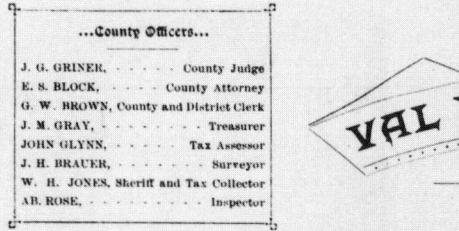

...County Officers...

J. G. GRINER,	County Judge
E. S. BLOCK,	County Attorney
G. W. BROWN,	County and District Clerk
J. M. GRAY,	Treasurer
JOHN GLYNN,	Tax Assessor
J. H. BRAUER,	Surveyor
W. H. JONES,	Sheriff and Tax Collector
AB. ROSE,	Inspector

...Commissioners...

LOUIS KIEFFER,	Precinct No. 1
ROBERT GREENWOOD,	Precinct No. 2
G. O. STRICKLAND,	Precinct No. 3
N. G. KING,	Precinct No. 4

Del Rio, Texas, 2/5— 1898

Sam is all Right of course he had to Kill a man who Beat him very Bad I did not Blame him and I went to Del Rio and Gave the Bond he is at home and all Right of cause it will caust Some money But That is all

Yours Truly
Roy Bean

With his practice of law as unorthodox as his character, "Judge" Roy Bean established his own brand of "law west of the Pecos" for twenty years. After finding $40 and a pistol on a dead man, he fined the deceased $40 for "carrying a concealed weapon." On another occasion, he released a man accused of killing an Oriental because he could not find in his law books where it was "against the law to kill a chinaman." In this 1898 letter from Texas, Bean wrote to his family about his brother: "Sam is all right. Of course he had to kill a man who beat him very bad. I did not blame him and I went to Del Rio and gave the bond. He is at home and all right. Of course it will cost some money, but that is all."

This cabinet card photo of Annie Oakley show the many medals she earned as a sharpshooter.

Light. Incandescent lighting does not harm documents, but both direct sunlight and fluorescent lighting are harmful to documents over a period of time. The ultraviolet rays cause documents to fade and yellow. Sunlight has altered the colors of dustjackets on books in my library because my bookcases were in a location that exposed them to sunlight.

Humidity. If you live in a region where humidity is high, your documents will suffer unless you take steps to correct it. High humidity promotes the growth of mold and other chemical reactions on papers. Store your document collection in a dry, cool place, preferably with a constant temperature around seventy degrees.

Glue Stains. These might appear on the back of documents mounted in a scrapbook or frame (known as "mounting traces"), or you might detect glue stains on the left border of stock certificates. It used to be common to return a cancelled stock to its issue book, glued to its original stub. Some stocks are sold with the stub attached; others have had the stub removed, sometimes leaving glue remnants. Little or nothing can be done to remove glue stains, so such documents must be accepted in this condition.

Cancellations and Other Marks

Excessive cancellation marks may affect a document's value. They appear primarily on financial-related documents, such as stocks, bonds, and checks, to show remittance of the document's value and to assure that it will not be used a second time.

Documents undergo various methods and types of cancellation. A "cut cancellation" produces razor-like cuts once or several times across the body of the document. "Bank-hammer cancellation" also cuts the document without removing any paper by using a large stapler-like device. A "punch cancellation" removes tiny bits of paper where small holes appear, often in various designs or sizes. Some punch cancellations produce words like PAID or CANCELLED on the document. Punch cancellations may affect a document's autographic value if the holes perforate a signature, which they sometimes intentionally do; if so, the document should be priced accordingly and in relation to how the cancellation affects the signature.

In retrospect, historic Fort Bridger in Wyoming perhaps should have been renamed "Fort Carter" after Judge William Carter, who settled at the post in 1857 and remained the authoritative figure there for over two decades. After making the post his home, Carter went on to become the post trader, postmaster, freighter, Wells Fargo agent, and judge. Note the embossed revenue stamp on the check with the bank-hammer cancellation mark on the left side of the stamp. On the right side of the stamp is a "PAID" stamped cancellation.

A "pen cancellation" occurs when someone writes PAID or CANCELLED or draws an X or wavy lines across the face or body of a document; unfortunately, these sometimes adversely affect the vignettes on stocks or bonds. "Stamp cancellations," made with an inked steel or rubber stamp, may also say PAID or CANCELLED and can detract from the beauty of the document if used excessively. Other business-related cancellation marks might use the words RECEIVED, DUE, or ACCEPTED, followed by the company's name and a date.

Avoid collecting documents with excessive cancellation marks on them. Some cancelled stocks and bonds look as though someone had riddled them with a machine gun. Generally, when a document's cancellation marks overpower its beauty or intrinsic value, it isn't worth collecting.

This 1883 western check has four connections to Indians: it is issued from Indian Territory; it was issued by the government-approved Indian trader; it has an Indian vignette; and it has been issued to the local Indian chief. Indian-related documents are scarce.

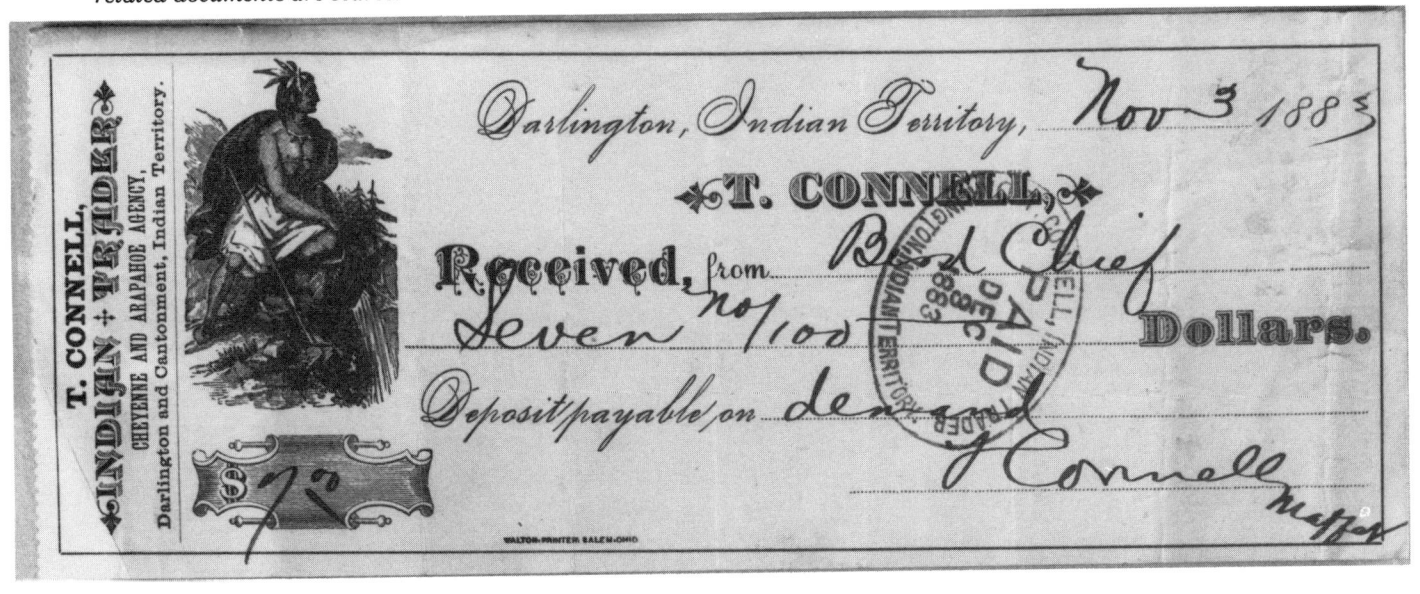

This 1885 bank draft from Tombstone, Arizona Territory, features ornate artwork. It has a 2-cent revenue tax stamp imprinted in the body with a cut-cancellation through it. Most financial documents receive cancellation marks to prevent them from being reused.

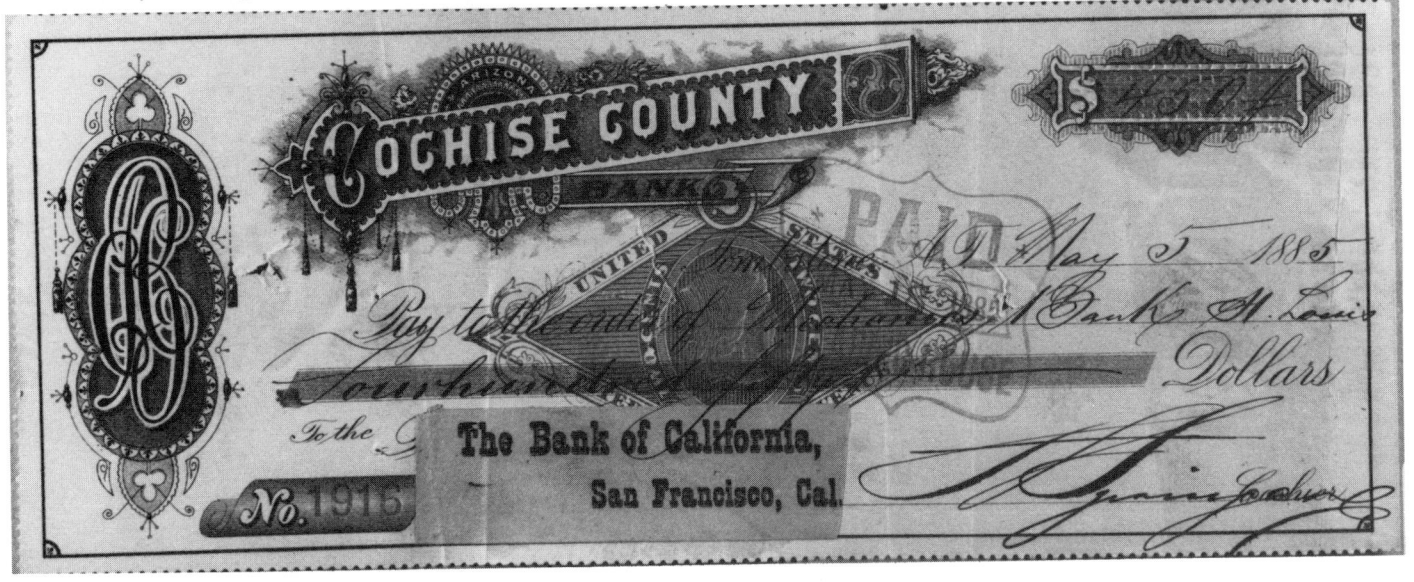

Revenue Stamps

When I first started collecting paper Americana, I noticed certain types of documents had stamps on them—some were printed on the document while others were moistened and affixed. I later learned that some of these "revenue stamps" are rare and may increase a document's value besides adorning it with color.

In 1862 the U.S. government began placing a taxation fee on certain types of business and financial documents to help offset the rising costs of the Civil War. The practice continued for two decades on such documents as bank checks or drafts, receipts, insurance deeds, express or telegraph documents, agreements, stocks and bonds, mortgages, deeds, and photographs.

Early revenue stamps are similiar in appearance to modern postal stamps. Gummed on the back for ease in affixing to documents, all those issued through 1873 bore an illustration of George Washington. The stamps came in various colors and denominations ranging from one cent to $500, although most common are those in the two-cent to $2 category. The taxing of certain documents continued until 1883, when the government rescinded the law.

Revenue stamps were cancelled usually by simply drawing a line in ink across the face; however, another form of cancellation—much harder to find these days—is the "hand-stamped" cancellation, a circular mark with the name of

This 1864 Comstock Lode mining stock from Nevada Territory is signed by William Stewart as president. Stewart was a sharp mining lawyer who served nearly two and a half decades as a U.S. senator from Nevada. His specialty as both lawyer and senator was serving the needs of California's "Big Four" and most notably C. P. Huntington and the Southern Pacific Railroad.

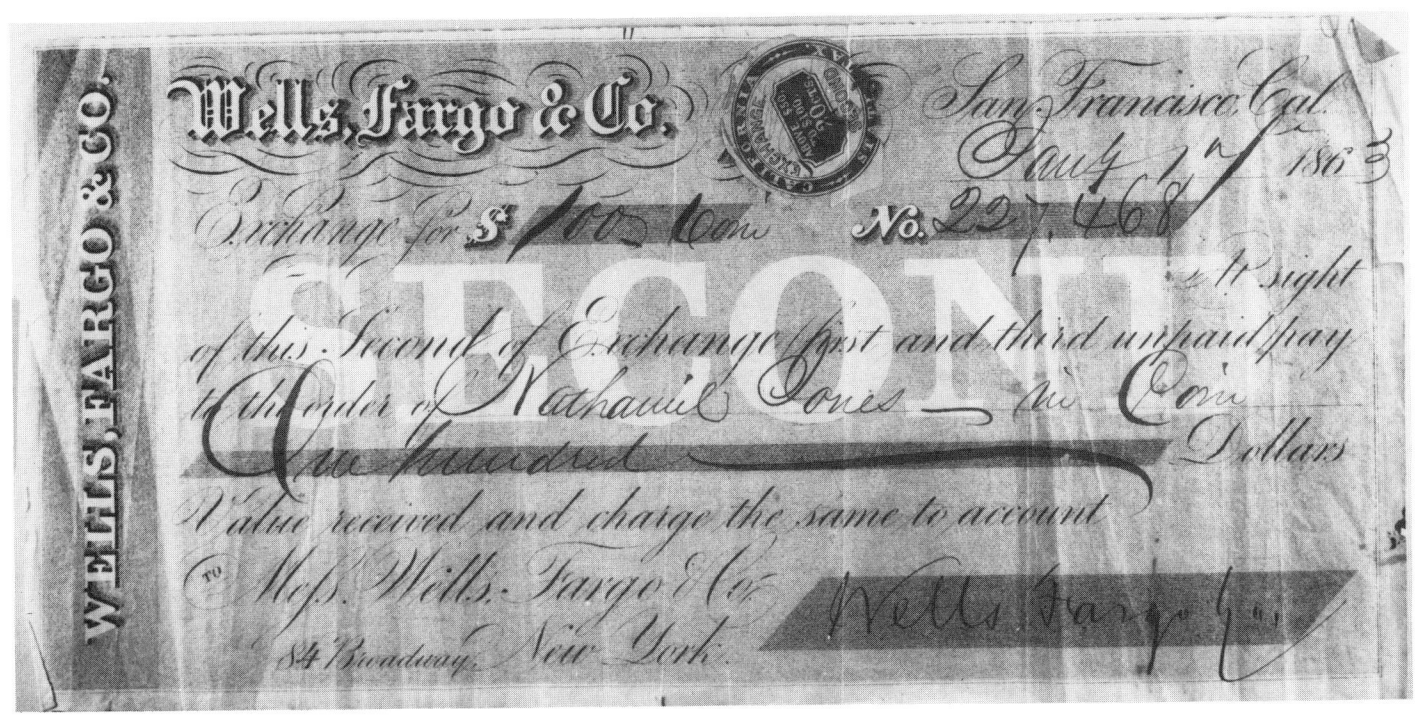

Dated 1863 from San Francisco, this Wells Fargo Second of Exchange has a scarce California stamp applied at the top.

Today's ghost town of Kingston, Nevada, was once a roaring mining camp. This mining receipt is a tangible piece of evidence from the camp's heyday. The receipt acknowledges payment for hauling freight to the camp. Note the 2-cent revenue stamp attached at the top.

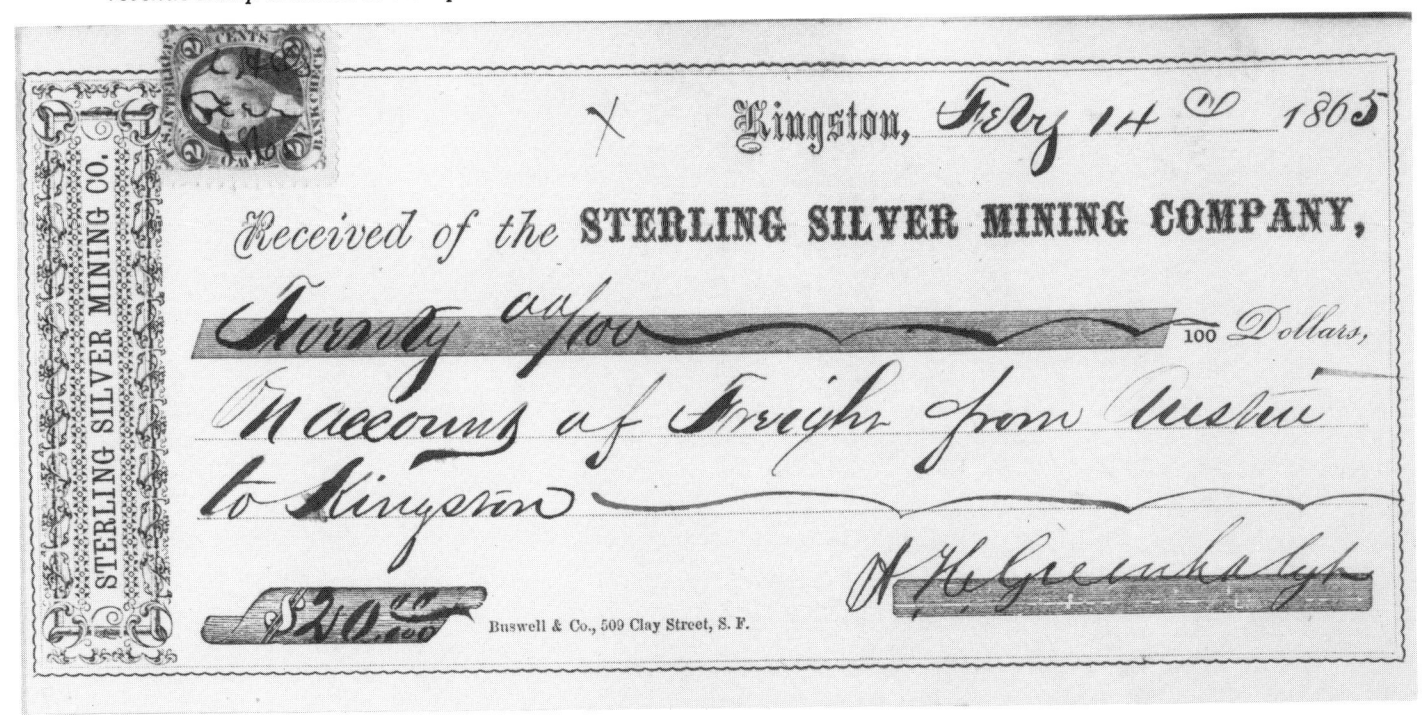

the business and the date. They look similiar to the postmarks seen on mail today.

The government renewed its revenue stamp program in 1898 to help pay mounting costs of the Spanish-American War by taxing certain financial and business documents. Unlike the earlier versions, these were known as "documentary stamps." The 1898-1901 series ranged in denominations from one-half cent to $50. Later variations and denominations of stamps were introduced in 1914 and continued to be used on fewer numbers of selected documents until 1967.

A series of revenue stamps specifically for stock certificates existed between 1918 and 1952. Known as "stock transfer stamps," they taxed the stock whenever it changed ownership or was cancelled. Stock transfer stamps were issued by the federal and some state governments.

A few western states and territories added their own tax stamps to certain documents in the 1860s and 1870s. Nevada revenue stamps appear on some financial documents; California issued one temporarily, and they are much harder to find.

The revenue stamps I've discussed so far have been of the lick-and-stick variety, like postage stamps; another type of revenue stamp was printed directly on financial documents. The imprinted revenue stamps also were used between 1862 and 1882 and again for a short time during the Spanish-American War in 1898. Their denominations ranged from two cents to a dollar, and they came in various colors, sizes, and illustrations. These revenue stamps also had various forms of cancellation marks on them, the most common being a cut-cancellation or bank-hammer cancellation, both of which cut a line or pattern into the revenue stamp without removing any paper.

Revenue stamps of both kinds can brighten and add to the overall attractiveness and value of the documents in your collection.

CHAPTER SEVEN
Establishing Your Collection

Before starting your own collection, study the marketplace and the various collecting fields, then decide what type of material you want to collect and chart your course. Do you want only western autographs? What subject areas, such as mining, railroads, banking, or cattle, stir your interest? Will you focus on documents from a particular state or territory? What years define the period you want to collect from? Are you interested only one type of document, or will you collect multiple types? The boundaries you can build into your collection are many.

My collection lacked boundaries when I first started collecting. For a couple of years I wandered as aimlessly as a ship without a rudder through the paper Americana marketplace. But, increasingly, my focus moved toward material from the western half of the United States between 1840 and 1910. Unfortunately, by the time I decided on these boundaries, I had already spent hundreds on documents that didn't fit them. I do not recommend this course for new collectors. Plan ahead, shop around, ask questions—before you buy.

Some collecters focus on one subject—perhaps mining, railroads, cattle, postal/express, or finance—then collect any interesting documents pertaining to that subject. Other people focus on several subjects, depending upon their interests. Still others are more eclectic—gathering whatever they find interesting or unique, and using nothing more than a general geographic area (the western states and territories, for example) as their boundary. Geography is one way to define the limits of your collection, such as collecting material from a particular state or town; or you can define your collection by both geography and subject, collecting only from a particular mining district or railroad line, for instance.

A Working Example, My Collection

I'm often asked what I personally collect and why. It's a fair question, and this is my opportunity to explain my own collecting interests and strategy. I strive for an even mixture of stock and bond certificates and documents.

Stock and Bond Certificates. One of the reasons I collect stocks and bonds is because they are among the most visually appealing documents in western history. The majority of available stocks and bonds came from the eastern half of the U.S. because that part of the country had been growing for two hundred years when westward expansion began in the mid-1800s. Of all the obsolete stocks and bonds on the market today, at least two-thirds of the issuing companies were incorporated or located in eastern states. Much of the financing for western development came from the East, so fewer "western" shares of stocks and bonds existed; yet, until recently, western stock certificates and bonds generally sold at the same prices as those from the East, even though they were rarer. This is all changing now. In the field of western stocks and bonds I focus on four areas: 1) mining, 2) railroads, 3) energy, and 4) general. I chose these areas for a number of reasons, but mostly because I wanted *western* documents.

1) *Mining:* In the western paper Americana market, mining and mining camps are a very popular collecting subject. Mining stock certifi-

One western character who led the life of a true adventurer was Albert J. Fountain. His extensive adventures and contributions to New Mexico Territory are well known. He fought Apaches in the Civil War and later served as a military scout. Fountain was a U.S. senator in Texas, but returned to New Mexico to practice law. He served as Billy the Kid's defense lawyer and later served as special prosecutor against cattle rustlers. In 1896, after charging some thirty men with cattle rustling, Fountain and his eight-year-old son were murdered, but their bodies were never found. Pat Garrett spent nearly three years searching for the killers and arrested three men who were later acquitted. Fountain tried his hand at numerous business ventures while in New Mexico, including a stint as president of his mining company.

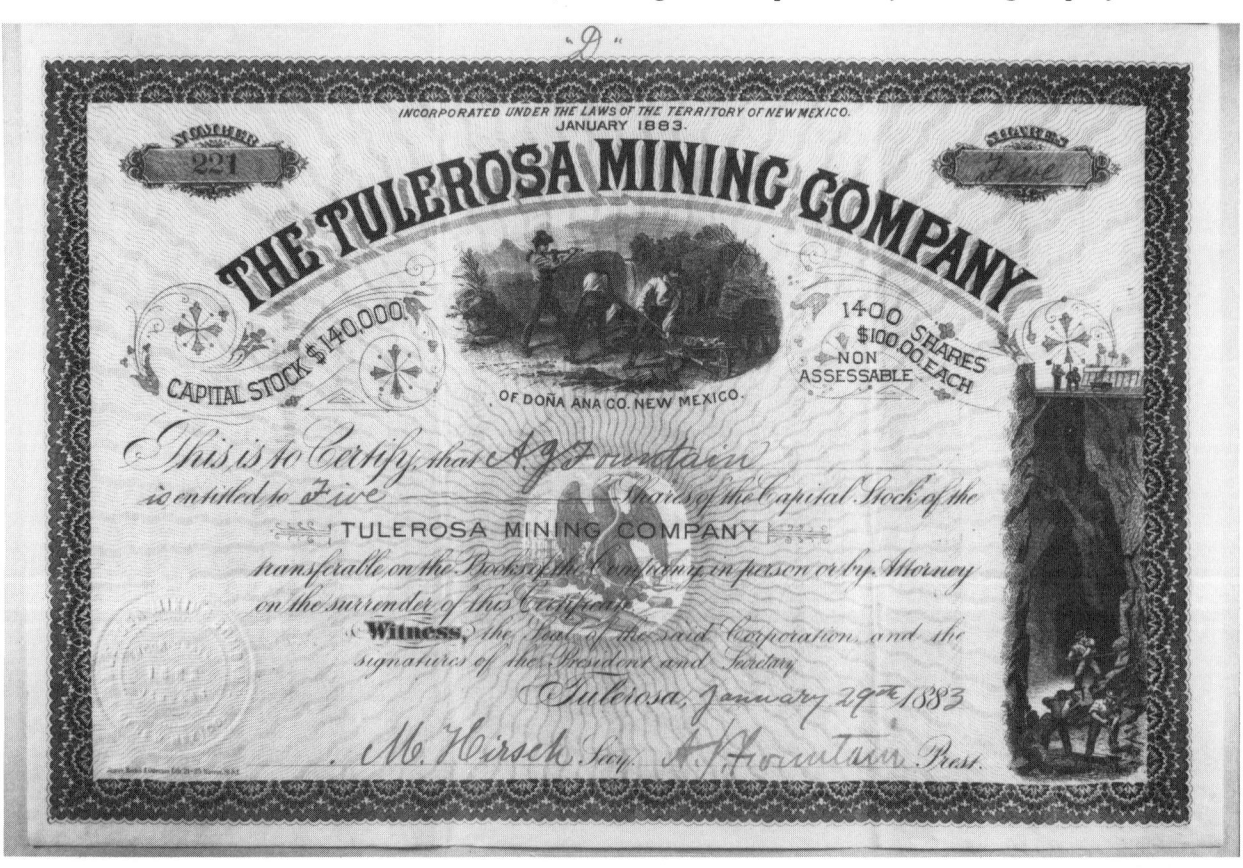

cates and bonds are among the most attractive documents you'll find in this field. Some certificates have autographic value, too. Others have unique or unusual artwork or may come from an obscure mining district. Anyone who has spent much time visiting some of the old ghost towns and mining camps in the West surely understands the allure of old western mining certificates. I collect only pre-1910 pieces—the more ornate, the better. At today's prices, you can buy nice-looking certificates for about $25; rarer pieces start around $75; and some of the earliest pieces from the 1850s and 1860s go for $150-$250 or more.

2) *Railroad:* Like mining, railroad stocks and bonds comprise another popular collecting subject in western paper Americana. The field changed some in the mid-1980s when hundreds of thousands of railroad certificates from several railroad archives flooded the marketplace, diluting it and changing the supply-and-demand ratios. Most of these came from eastern railroad companies; in 1900, 70 percent of all railroad tracks in the United States were east of the Missouri River. Far fewer western than eastern railroad certificates exist, and in most cases they are harder to find. Like western mining certificates, railroad stocks and bonds may have auto-

Early western railroad stocks and bonds are harder to find than their eastern counterparts. By 1900 over 70 percent of all U.S. railroad lines were still east of the Missouri River. This 1880 stock is for a short line between Kansas and Nebraska. Note the quality printing by the American Bank Note Company.

graphic value, but rare examples are harder to find, so I allow more time to collect pre-1920 pieces. Western railroad certificates start at $25-$50; rarer pieces sell for $100-$200; some bonds from the 1850s and 1860s go for $300-$500.

3) *Energy:* Development of the oil, coal, gas, and electric industries in the West has been primarily a twentieth century enterprise. Prior to 1900, western energy did not go beyond sporadic production at the regional level due to difficult transportation to energy fields, the lack of public demand, and inadequate shipping. Then came the giant oil strike at Spindletop, Texas, in 1901, and other strikes soon after in California. These ushered in the age of automobiles and a desire to develop other energy sources.

Oil stocks are the most abundant of the four energy groups; however, pre-1900 oil stocks from the West are very rare. By state, the earliest oil stocks in my collection are: California, 1886; Colorado, 1897; Oregon, 1901; Texas, 1900; Utah, 1901; Wyoming, 1901; other certificates in my collection are pre-1910. Early gas, coal, and electric stocks are difficult to find, especially those dating before 1900. If you are interested in collecting in this field, focus on pre-1920 pieces. Unlike mining and railroad certificates, energy certificates seldom have autographic value. Apparently, more men became famous and made their millions from mining and railroads than from energy production.

4) *General Stocks and Bonds:* In my collection, these certificates are those *not* from mining, railroads, or energy. I enjoy finding uncommon, unusual, and unique western stocks and bonds. Some interesting companies around the West have peddled stock to promote business. I have certificates on banking, transportation, town sites, cattle, communications, lumber, and a few stock-fraud issues thrown in for good measure.

The petroleum industry was founded in the early 1860s in Pennsylvania. Soon it spread to the West Coast, where promoters and entreprenuers first tried to develop oil fields. This 1889 oil stock from Monterey County, California, is one of the earliest western oil stocks issued. The vignette depicts oil derricks, storage tanks, and barrels—all built from wood!

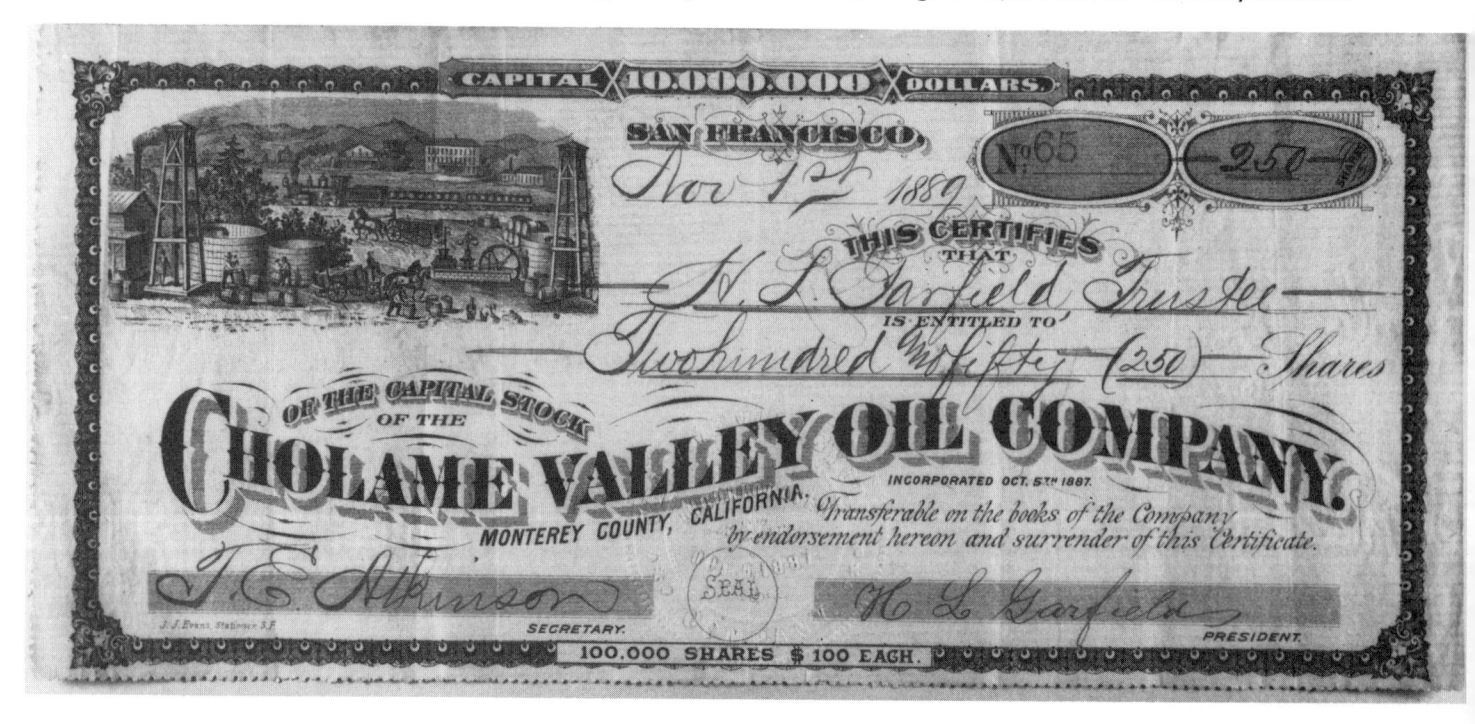

—72—

Most date before 1910. Some are oddball pieces, such as a 1908 Arizona stock for the "Thornless Cactus Farming Company" and a 1914 stock for "The Nevada Kid: Feature Film Producing Company." Patient searching will yield you some historical and colorful certificates.

Documents. The document half of my collection also breaks into four areas of personal interest: 1) autographs, 2) military/fort documents, 3) finance, and 4) general western documents.

1) *Autographs:* Collecting western autographs requires a bigger wallet, but it is also one of the most exciting and financially rewarding fields in terms of collector value. Western autographs usually start around $100, with the most important signatures going for $5,000-$10,000. My collection has only a few big names; most are of lesser-known Westerners who nevertheless made important contributions to western history.

2) *Military/Fort Documents:* This overlooked and undervalued collecting area literally did not exist in 1980, and very few dealers offer them still. The military documents in my collection date between 1850 and 1890. Many come from little-known posts or have historical content or signatures of heroic cavalry and infantrymen. I also have documents from over fifty posts, forts, camps, and a few places "in the field."

Eighty-eight western criminals met their fate at the gallows of Fort Smith, Arkansas, on the decision of "Hanging Judge" Issac Parker between 1876 and 1896. Sixty-five lawmen also died during this same period enforcing the law in Indian Territory (Oklahoma), over which Judge Parker had authority. This oath of office is signed by U.S. Marshal V. A. Morris and Parker.

Final Statement of _David Young_, a private of Captain _S. J. Norvell's_ Company [_M_] of the _Tenth_ Regiment of _Cavalry_, born in _Waynesboro'_, in the State of _South Carolina_ aged _26_ years, _five_ feet _six_ inches high, _Black_ complexion, _Black_ eyes, _Black_ hair, and by occupation a _Laborer_, was enlisted by _Major Jones_ at _Boston, Mass._, on the _Fourth_ day _September_, eighteen hundred and _Sixty Seven_, to serve for _five_ years, who is now entitled to a discharge by reason of _Expiration of term of Service_

The said _Private David Young_ was last paid by Paymaster _J. W. Nichols_ to include the _thirty first_ day of _August_, eighteen hundred and _seventy two_, and has pay due from that time to this present date.

He has been drawing $ ____ per mo. for ____ years' continuous service under sec. 2, act Aug. 4, '54.
There is due to him _Sixty Six ($66 30/100)_ — $\frac{30}{100}$ dollars retained pay.
There is due to him _____ $\frac{}{100}$ dollars bounty.
There is due to him _Six ($6 09)_ — $\frac{09}{100}$ dollars on account of clothing not drawn in kind.
He is indebted to the United States _____ $\frac{}{100}$ dollars on account of extra clothing.
He is indebted to the United States _____
He is indebted to _____, laundress of Company ____, _____ Regiment of _____ $\frac{}{100}$ dollars.
The cost of the ration at this post is _____ cents.
Remarks: _____

I CERTIFY that the above Final Statement, given in duplicate at _Fort Sill, I. T._, this _Fourth_ day of _September_, 1872, is correct.

S. J. Norvell
Captain 10th Cavalry
Commanding Company.

[A. G. O. No. 94.]

Black men who joined the Union Army following the Civil War usually enlisted for five years. In 1872, twenty-six-year-old Private David Young received his discharge from the military at Fort Sill, Indian Territory, after serving five years.

3) *Finance:* This category contains documents used in financial transactions and includes checks, bank drafts, currency, state and territorial warrants, certificates of deposit, and pay orders. Many have revenue stamps or vignettes on them. My financial documents are not always bank related; some are from mining, transportation, military, or railroads.

4) *General Documents:* This is a varied lot on a variety of subjects. I own a number of pre-1900 letters with good content, some with interesting and ornate letterheads. I also have some law enforcement/judicial documents signed by judges, sheriffs, and marshals, as well as a wide range of transporation documents. In addition, I've collected various attractive documents and a few broadsides/broadsheets relating to Indians, mining, cattle, oil, and banking.

All the above-mentioned categories, then, comprise my collecting parameters. I hope this helps give you an idea of how a working collection might range. After you settle on one or more collecting subjects, consider what time frame you wish to collect from and what sort of regional or geographic boundaries should apply to your collection. This book focuses primarily on documents from 1840 to 1910; with few exceptions, I recommend that serious collectors acquire only pre-1910 material.

As you plan and build your collection, try to avoid excessively restrictive boundaries. Occasionally collectors ask me for such specialized items that neither I nor anyone I can think of could help them. If you want something that simply can't be found in the marketplace, you'll soon become discouraged. Keep your boundaries flexible enough to change along with your collecting interests.

Caring for Your Collection

One of the most important aspects of collecting historical documents is properly caring for and preserving your collection to ensure its survival and value in the future. Each document that deteriorates further while you or I own it impoverishes both our society and us as collectors and caretakers of our past.

As with fine art, coins, or any other valuable collectibles, proper care is vital. Over the years we have learned some important dos and don'ts that can help assure a long, safe life for your collection. Ignoring these tips could result in damage to your documents and devaluation of your collection. If you're going to invest time, effort, and money to start a collection, you must learn how to take care of it.

Until the late 1970s most dealers and collectors were generally naive about adequate and appropriate storage of their collections and inventories. Before then, very little information had been available to the public about the care and conservation of old documents and manuscripts. Only archivists and curators at libraries, museums, universities, and other institutions seemed to care about preserving historical papers. This information deficit among private dealers and collectors resulted in improper storage and handling of material for a number of years; and those who wanted better care often had no access to archival supplies.

To illustrate how we must each be careful in obtaining the right supplies, I'll tell you about one of my experiences. During my first year or two as a dealer I met another dealer at a show who sold 11"x14" display books to house paper collectibles. Each clear page had a black paper insert. When I asked, the dealer assured me the pages were acid-free; he also used the books to display and sell his own inventory, so I accepted his word and bought some for my collection. But I kept wondering if they really were safe. Finally I decided to get some confirmation.

I sent a sample display page and paper insert to an archival supply firm for analysis. They told me the black paper inserts were "highly acidic," and they suspected the clear plastic pages of having a petroleum base, which would have made them acidic as well. It shocked me to discover that my collection was slowly being poisoned. I sent photocopies of my lab analysis to the dealer, who claimed ignorance and said he would stop selling the display books, but his advertisement for the display books kept running in each issue of a publication for paper money collectors.

Several months later I wrote to the advertising manager of the publication and asked for his help in protecting the collections of his subscribers who might buy these display books. Eventually, after intense lobbying on my part, the publishers got the dealer to run a small disclaimer in his ad stating that items stored in the display books "might" be harmed by "lengthy exposure" to the pages and inserts. I decided the publication was more interested in its advertisers than its subscribers. These display books are still on the market. I don't know what long-term effects they may have on the documents inside them, but continued exposure to the acids is bound to accelerate deterioration of the paper fibers and will perhaps lead to other problems as well.

Unfortunately, many paper Americana collectors shop at regular office supply or variety stores where they can buy clear viewing pages that fit into standard three-ring binders cheaply. Some brands have black paper inserts. Though inexpensive, these clear viewing pages likely are made with petroleum-based vinyl or plastic, which makes them unsuitable for storing historical documents. Do not use these or inexpensive photographs albums with sticky pages that hold photographs in place.

Of course, the reason for buying such things as display books is to minimize the handling of unprotected documents. When you do handle your paper collectibles, make sure your hands are clean and free of natural oils or moisture. And always keep drinks of all sorts away from where you are examining documents.

Several archival supply houses in the United States offer quality, acid-free display books and other preservation and archival supplies to both private collectors and institutions. The problem is hooking up collectors with the right suppliers. Two I recommend as worth contacting for more information are:

Light Impressions
439 Monroe Avenue
Rochester, NY 14607-3717

University Products
517 Main Street
Holyoke, MA 01041

Since the mid-1980s a new type of clear viewing page has become popular with collectors. The pages are made with polyproplyene, an inert, safe, acid-free thermo-resin; it will not change, crack, or discolor under normal use. Polyproplyene has no plasticizers in it and does not cause static electricity. It contains most of the qualities found in more expensive archival viewing pages. If you install paper inserts in the viewing pages, be sure to use rigid, acid-free, buffered card stock.

You may wish to frame and display some of your prized pieces in your home or office. If so, consider a few important things first, and do the job right. I have made my share of mistakes while teaching myself about this, since virtually nothing was available when I first started. Based on my experience, I offer you the following guidelines.

First, don't do it yourself. Trust your collectibles to professionals at the framing shop or art gallery. You can choose the frame and matting materials and discuss what you want the framer to do, but let the expert take over from there.

Second, use non-glare glass instead of regular glass. It costs a little more but will more effectively spare your document from harmful types of direct light. If you have a very expensive piece, you may opt to frame it with a form of plexiglass sold under several trade names that protects your document from ultraviolet or florescent lights.

Third, select an acid-free matt at the frame shop to create a border around your document so the glass won't touch it. Make sure the backing paper behind the document is also acid-free.

Fourth, never place your framed documents in direct sunlight. Be careful to keep papers on your desk or table out of the sunlight as it shifts across the room during the day. Indirect light or incandescent lighting will not harm your documents, but direct sunlight will discolor them, and long-term flourescent lighting can cause them to fade.

Always protect your documents, framed or not, from excessive heat and humidity. Sometimes this is hard to do, but, as a general rule, keep your collection in a cool, dry place, out of direct sunlight. Store it in a safe room with a stable temperature, preferably around 70 degrees F. The ideal relative humidity for your collection is 50 percent, but it can tolerate 70 percent humidity without adverse effects; if you live in a climate where the humidity often exceeds or dips below this range, consider investing in either a dehumidifier or a humidifier, as appropriate. Avoid storing your collection in a hot, stuffy attic or a cold, damp basement.

When the value of your collection starts running into four figures, it's time to insure it against theft, fire, or any other loss. In anticipation of that time, keep your sales receipts and compile an accurate list of all the items in your collection, including what you bought (type of document, brief description, condition), when you bought it, from whom, and how much you paid for it. Update your list as often as necessary, and take it with you when you decide to buy insurance.

An inexpensive and effective way of documenting your collection is to make a photocopy or take a photograph of each document as soon as you acquire it. Keep the photocopies or photographs, your collection list, and sales receipts in a safe place.

Your standard homeowner's policy may adequately cover the value of your collection, depending upon the type of coverage you have. The drawback of using a standard homeowner's policy, however, is that your collections or antiques are figured simply as personal property without consideration of their real value in the event of a loss. This could create a problem in reimbursement if your collection is destroyed or stolen. Some companies may require an appraisal of your collection before insuring it.

If your homeowner's policy doesn't provide adequate protection, you may need a "floater" policy that extends the coverage of your personal property. Find out which floater is best suited to your needs, and be prepared to provide the insurance agent with the proper documentation. The agent may even wish to examine the collection.

The Future of Your Collection

No matter what you collect, eventually you have to face the fact that you can't take it with you. For an appropriate return on the time, effort, and money you'll invest in your collection, figure on building it over at least ten years before selling it. Plan the sale and its proper execution well ahead of time to maximize your profit. If you sell your collection within the first year or two, you're liable to take a loss.

Some options you may want to consider:

The Family Collection. Some collectors never consider selling their collections. They build them for posterity and hope the collection will continue to thrive and grow under family stewardship. Before this notion becomes concrete in your mind, consider some important criteria to turning over the fruits of your labor to one of your children or another family member.

First, be sure the recipient is worthy. Is the the candidate interested in acquiring the collection? Does he or she understand the collecting field? Will this person be a cautious caretaker of the collection? Can you be assured that the recipient won't sell part or all of it if this is not your wish? Consider these and other questions before making your decision. You should feel good about the disposition of your collection and confident that your family will continue to enjoy it, add to it, and take proper care of it.

When you decide to leave your collection to a family member, record your wishes in writing in a legally binding will to avoid any misunderstandings. Verbal intentions are too unspecific and could result in hard feelings among family member and, ultimately, allow a court to decide the fate of your collection.

Institutional Donation. You may wish to donate your collection to a museum, library, or university. If this is the case, consider how well your collection might fit into a particular special-collections theme the institution might have; a good fit may inspire better care. Make sure the institution has the proper storage (or display) facilities and ample staff who are interested in your collection and will see that it gets proper care and management. Would you allow the institution ever to sell your collection? If so, to whom and under what conditions? To assure that the institution keeps and displays the collection according to your wishes, put your intentions in writing, along with any provisions or conditions (such as not banishing it to the dark confines of an inaccessible back room). If taxes are among your considerations, you'll probably need an appraisal of your collection and the advice of a tax attorney.

Auction. This can be a convenient way to dispose of your collection. You simply turn it over to an auction house and let them handle everything in exchange for a commission of 10-25 percent. The exciting thing about an auction is that your collection lots will be sold to the highest bidder rather than at a fixed price. On the down side, though, there's the possibility that a lot might sell for less than its estimated value, or possibly not sell at all.

There are many variables in an auction; it is imperative that you consign your collection to the right auction or auctions. Turning it over to an auction firm that doesn't specialize in documents could put you at a serious disadvantage. The best return may come from breaking up your collection among several auctions that specialize in certain types of documents.

The thought of their historical documents being enjoyed by other collectors in perpetuity appeals to most collectors. Knowing that your collection (or its parts) will remain in the public marketplace and will continue to interest the public and increase its awareness of historical western documents can be very rewarding. The documents you own today can serve as tangible pieces of history for future generations to admire and interpret.

Direct Sale. Another outlet for selling your collection is doing so directly to dealers or other collectors. Unlike an auction, which could take months before you receive payment, selling your collection directly to individuals is faster and sometimes more profitable. Ideally, of course, you'll find another collector willing to pay full value for all or part of your collection.

I suggest the following three guidelines to make this course as easy as one, two, three:

First, prepare a descriptive listing of the items for sale. Avoid making the descriptions too brief; allow each item the space it needs for proper identification. Provide dates, colors, sizes, signatures, and any other pertinent information, including defects.

Second, identify as many potential buyers as you can and send each of them a letter explaining your intention to sell. If your list of items for sale is not too lengthy, enclose a copy of it along with the cover letter you are sending to the buyers. You may also decide to place classified ads in a few carefully selected collector publications (magazines and newsletters, for instance). Make photocopies of your documents to send to any potential buyers who request one. You might list your selling prices, or you can opt to accept the "highest offer" on the collection or individual items.

Third, get your money before you release possession of the documents, and, when sending anything in the mail, package it securely and insure it. If the buyer owes you a large sum of money, request a cashier's check or money order; if the sum is smaller and you've agreed to accept a personal check, wait for it to clear before mailing out the items. Show respect for the buyer's new possession by packing it securely to prevent damaged during shipping; how you package the item can make the difference between a happy transaction and a sour deal. If the value is substantial, insure the package. Overnight express delivery may have its advantages as well.

However you choose eventually to dispose of your collection—whether passing it along to your family, donating it to an institution, selling it at auction, or selling directly—record your intentions fully and clearly at your earliest convenience to avoid any mix-up in case of unforseen circumstances.

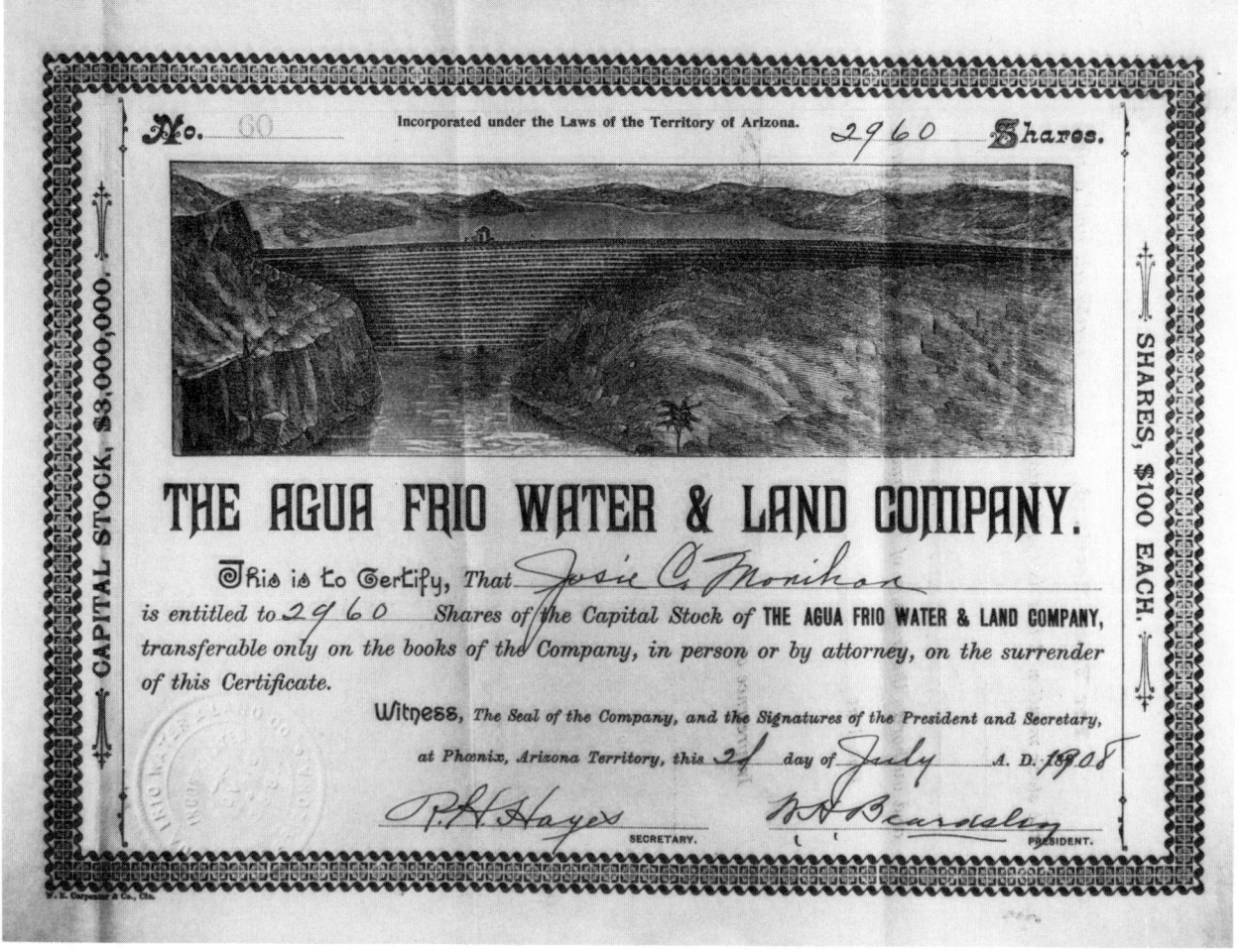

This Arizona Territory stock represents the region's most precious commodity—water. The aridity and heat of the Southwest account largely for the belated colonization of Arizona and New Mexico. As a result they did not become states until the twentieth century. The unusual vignette on this stock features an earthen dam built in the early 1900s to supply the growing community of Phoenix with precious water. This single certificate for 2,960 shares represents almost 10 percent of the company's entire stock.

Because Brigham Young opposed mining, pre-1880 mining stocks from Utah Territory are hard to find. This 1878 stock for the Atlanta Mining Company is the oldest I know of from the Tintic District and features an unusual vignette of Atlas lifting the world.

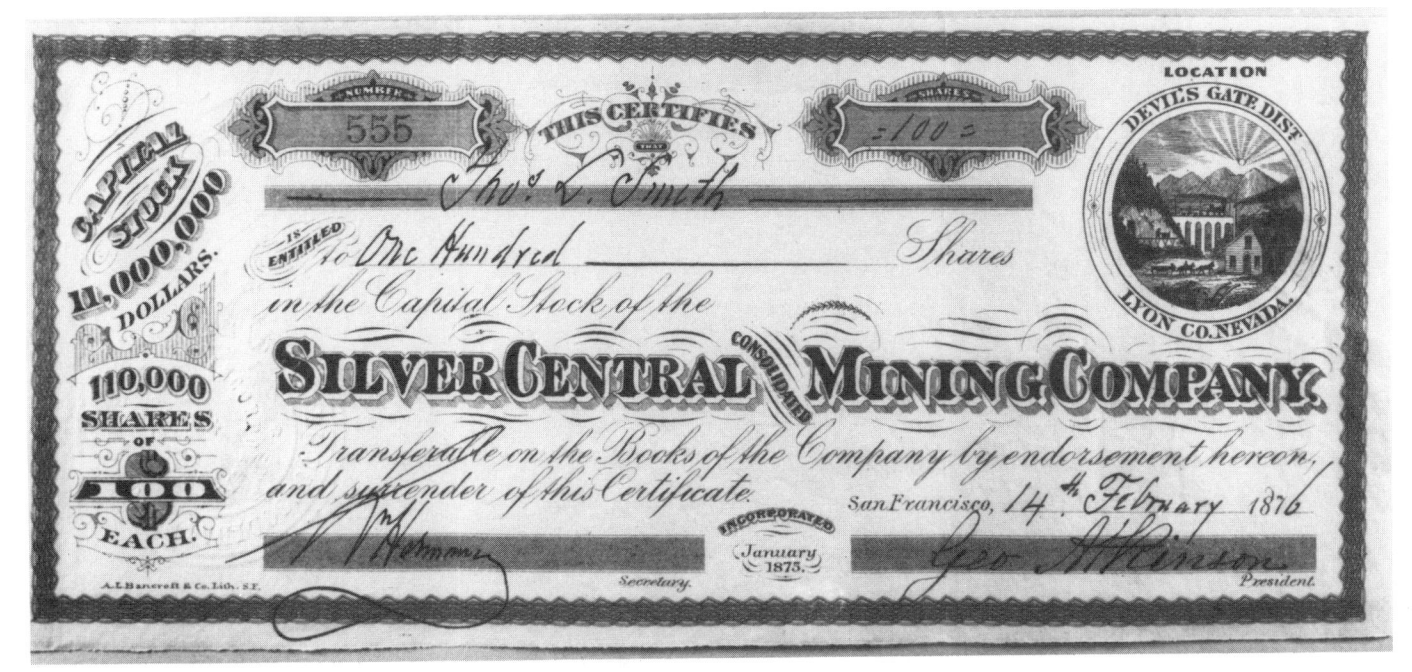

Stock certificates range in size from that of a dollar bill (2½"x6") to 10"x13" or larger. This 1876 Nevada mining stock measures about 4"x9"; the company's mines were located in the Devil's Gate District.

Gold Creek, Nevada, quickly flourished into a community of 1,000 miners, but it lasted only until they emptied the creek of its gold. The community experienced several booms and busts between 1873 and 1905, then it became a ghost town. The handsome vignette and quality printing assured shareholders that their investments were sound.

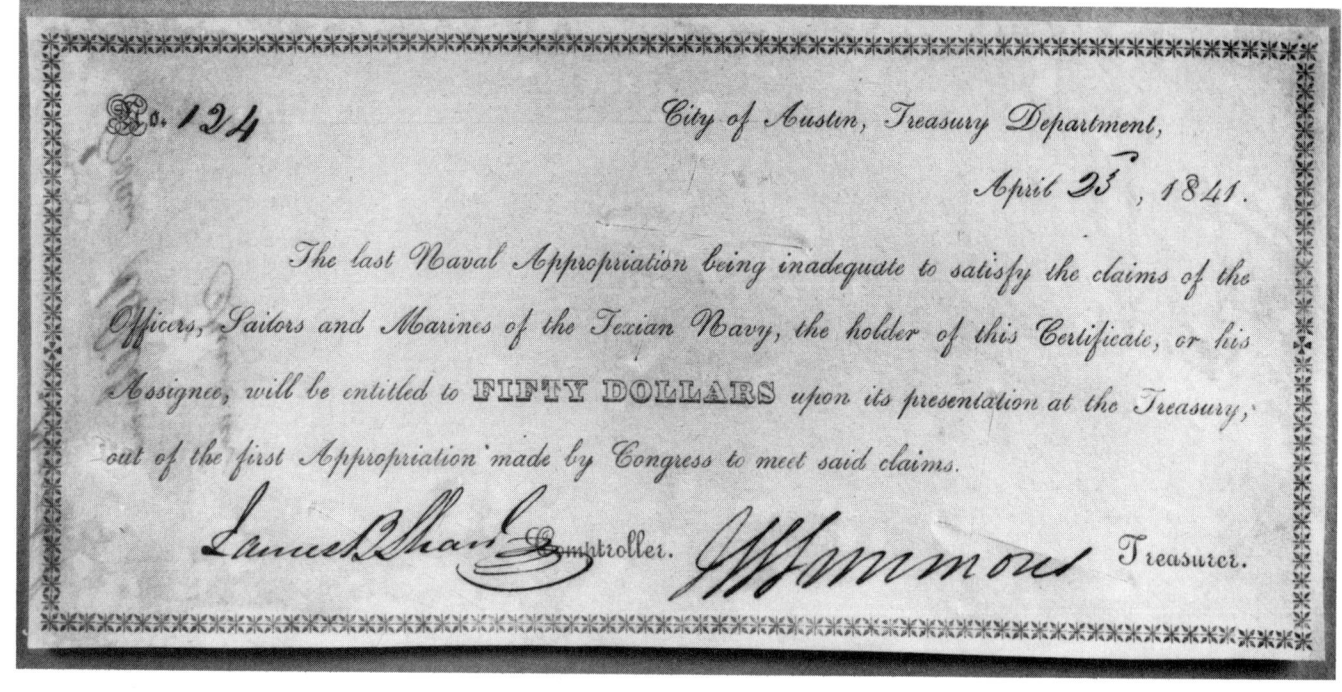

It's hard to imagine that the Republic of Texas had its very own navy, but here's proof—an 1841 pay warrant for $50. The Republic of Texas lasted only nine years before its admittance to the Union. Documents related to the "Texian Navy" are indeed hard to find.

This receipt from Virginia City, Nevada—site of the famous Comstock Lode—shows that the Savage Mining Company shipped three bars of silver bullion valued at $5,000 to San Francisco. It is signed at the bottom by a Wells Fargo agent.

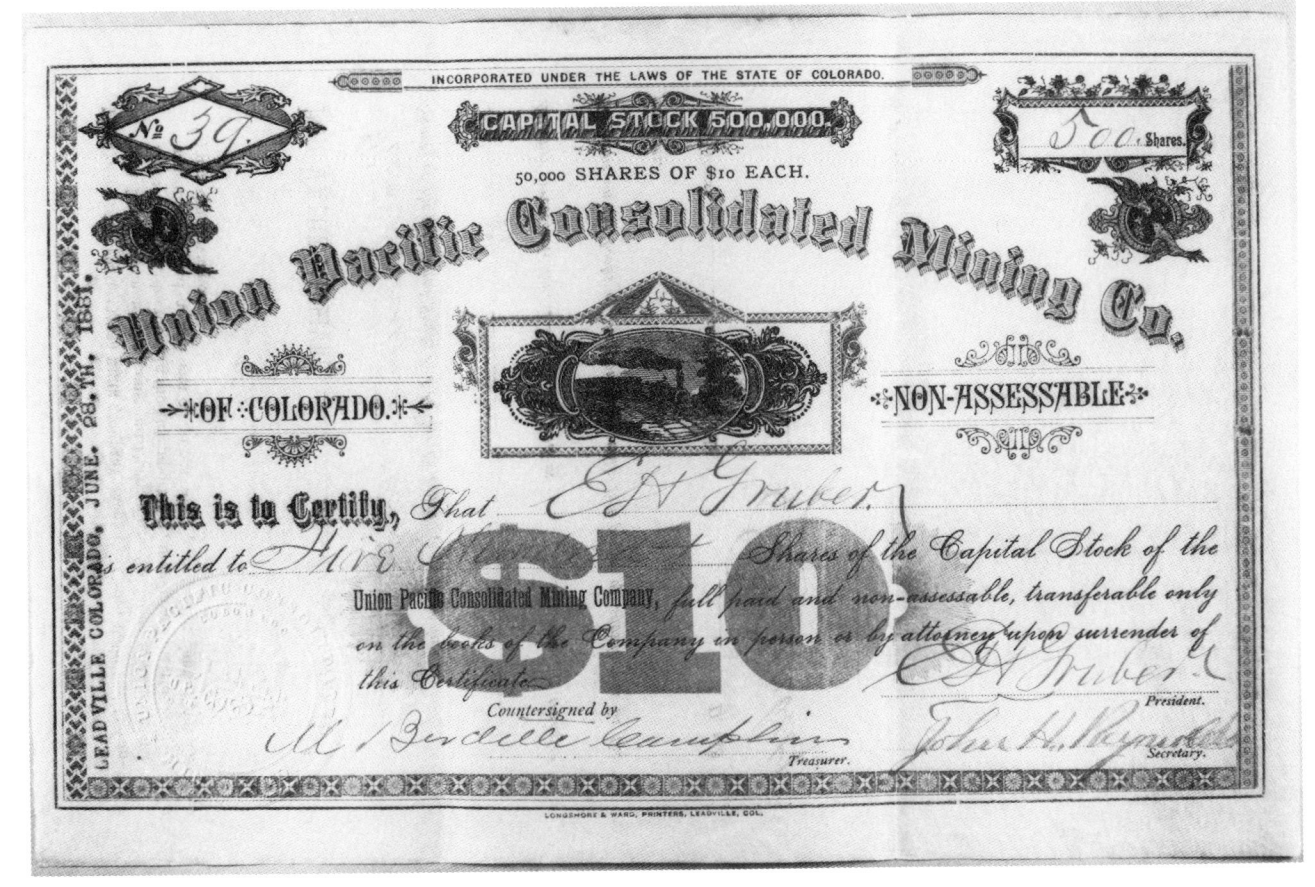

Some early mining stock promoters used dubious means to sell their stock. The Union Pacific Mining Company of Leadville, Colorado, attached itself to the famous railroad of the same name and used a train vignette and embossed seal of a locomotive to give shareholders the impression that the railroad supported the mining company. This was not true, however, and the Union Pacific Railroad sued the mining company over the misuse of their name, derailing the stock promoter's plans to get rich quick.

The area near Virginia City, Montana Territory, was the site of Montana's first gold rush in the early 1860s. This 1873 forwarding receipt shows a shipment by Wells Fargo of $4,000 in coinage to New York from Virginia City.

This 1864 mining stock certificate represents the first organized mining venture in Utah Territory. The company incorporated in California because Utah had no mining laws at the time. Its president, the anti-Mormon Gen. Patrick Edward Conner, encouraged prospecting near Salt Lake in the hope of launching a mining rush that would flood Utah with miners and break the Mormons' monoplistic hold on the territory. The stock's original owner, Nat Stein, was a business associate of stagecoach king Ben Holliday.

Stock certificates from the Old West rarely date earlier than this 1855 example from California. Originally issued from the mining camp of "Mormon Island," it has been crossed out and replaced with "Dotan's Bar." Only 600 shares in this company existed. The site of Dotan's Bar now lies at the bottom of Folsom Lake.

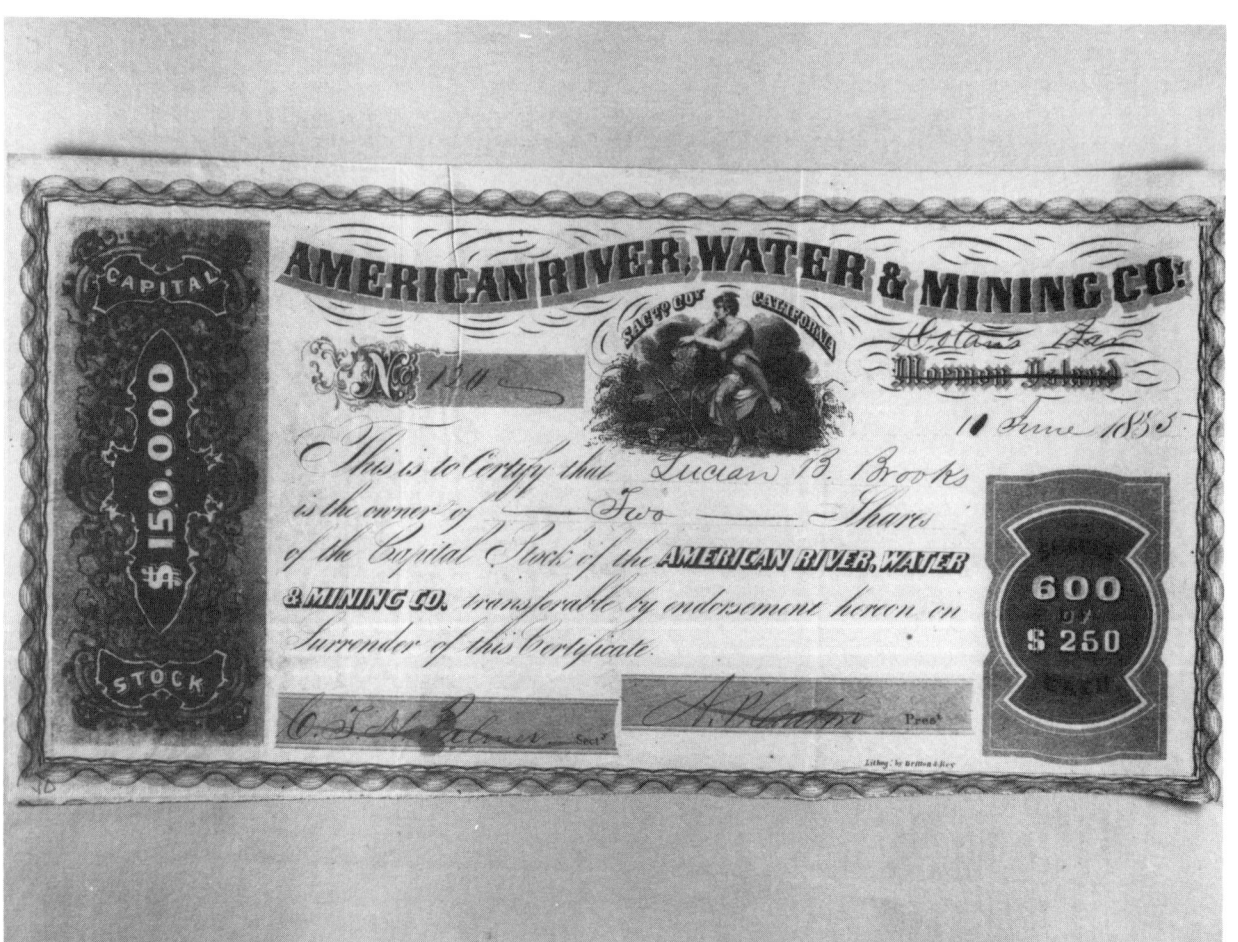

Issued only a few days after the O.K. Corral shootout, this 1881 stock for the Tombstone Mill & Mining Company is the only known bank-note printed stock of this vintage from Tombstone.

This 1896 mining stock, issued to and signed by David Moffat as president, represents but one of the mining, railroad, and banking magnate's many holdings. Long-time president of Denver's First National Bank and builder of railroads, Moffat wanted to punch a seven-mile long railroad tunnel through the Rocky Mountains between Denver and Salt Lake. The project began in 1902 and drained Moffat's assets. He died in 1911. Upon completion of the railroad, in 1928, the project engineers named the tunnel appropriately after Moffat.

CHAPTER EIGHT

Nearly Everything You Want to Know About Auctions and Dealers

As you prepare to begin your search for historical western documents, remember this: No two dealers or auctions are alike. Their terms of sale, guarantees, policy on refunds, auction rules, grading systems, and other business practices will vary.

Most of your purchases will come from dealer and auction catalogs. Spend your first six months getting a feel for the collecting market by joining several organizations and subscribing to some catalogs from dealers and auction firms. Before long you'll find some reliable dealers and collectors who can help you build your collection.

Always study the terms of sale before you buy. Try to find a dozen dealers and auction houses that offer the type of material you want so you can compare often and make the best purchases possible. While you will probably run into many scarce, one-of-a-kind documents, remember, too, that some documents, especially of the financial variety, are available in quantity. Documents known to exist in quantity should be priced accordingly; unfortunately, this is not always the case in catalogs. When in doubt, ask.

A few years ago I visited an elderly widow who wanted to sell some old stock certificates her late husband had collected. His real interest had been in philatelics. But he didn't share his hobby with his wife, so she knew nothing about stamps. He told her, though, that his stamp collection was worth $20,000, and that if he should die, she should sell the collection in an auction conducted by the stamp dealer through whom he had purchased much of his collection. The widow contacted the stamp dealer and he auctioned the collection for her. But she didn't get $20,000; she got just $2,000. The shock of the incident left her wiser, but $18,000 poorer.

Fortunately, this story is not representative of how auctions normally go. I know stories with happier financial endings. But my experiences, both as a bidder and consignor, with a dozen different auction houses range from rewarding to revolting. Auctions have advantages and disadvantages. Being aware of the potential obstacles and knowing how to avoid them should make your transactions with auction firms pleasant, rewarding, and productive.

Advice to Bidders

The best favor you can do yourself as a bidder is to review the auction rules closely before placing any bid. In addition to studying the terms of sale, read the terms and agreements from the auction. Some terms are lengthy and complex and may have additional charges to bidders in small print. Some auctions sell lots "as is" without guarantees. Autograph collectors should be extra cautious of "as is" signatures that may have been signed *for* someone rather than by that person. Auction rules may vary widely from one house to another, and understanding how the rules govern the auction and using them properly can work to your advantage.

A few years ago a large San Francisco auction firm that traditionally auctioned art and antiques conducted a western paper Americana auction. The firm did not have its own shipping department but contracted the service through another company. Although the firm explained this in its catalog, nowhere did it list shipping charges. I soon found out how much it cost, though, when the invoice for the dozen lots I purchased added $40 for shipping to my total. Including insurance, the shipping shouldn't have cost more than $10.

I contacted the shipper and learned that they were more accustomed to handling larger shipments of art, furniture, and other antiques from the auction firm. Large or small, the shipping contract with the auction firm remained the same. Luckily I had bought enough lots to more easily absorb the shipping costs. Another collector complained of a similar problem from this auction; since he won only one lot, his shipping bill exceeded the price of his purchase.

Most paper Americana auctions list their goods in catalogs and conduct bidding through the mail. The larger auctions held in major cities have live bidders in attendance, but they also mail out catalogs and accept bids by mail or over the phone.

Many auctions print the realized prices on all lots sold in their next auction catalog or in a special flyer. It's worth taking the time to study what the lots actually sell for in relation to their estimates. Doing so can help you identify trends in the market.

Most auctions add a 10 percent "buyer's charge" or "premium" to the winning bid. If the winning bid is $100, the 10 percent premium increases the total owed by the lot winner to $110. Unfortunately, it's just part of the cost of doing business at auctions. And they are generally very good places to find valuable material at reasonable prices. Some of my best pieces have come from auctions.

For a nominal fee, some auctions will provide photocopies of the lots for sale. This is a worthwhile service that can help you decide how high to bid. Other auctions may actually mail lots out for inspection prior to the bidding. Auctions in major cities usually allow you to preview the lots ahead of time. All these opportunities are worth taking advantage of whenever you can.

Some auctions provide a "Total Limit" clause, allowing you to bid on as many items as you wish with the understanding that your winning lots won't exceed your "total limit." If you have only $300 to bid, for instance, but you see six lots worth $700 you want to bid on, you can bid on all six lots with the understanding that your winning bids won't total more than $300. This increases your chances of getting what you want and not leaving the auction empty-handed.

Advice to Consigners

Some collectors consign materials they want to sell to an auction firm, confident that the auctioneer will get a good price from the highest bidder. For this, the auction firm will charge a consignment fee ranging usually from 10 percent to 25 percent, depending upon the size and value of the consignment. It is important that you match the type of material you have with the right kind of auction. Don't consign your documents in a book auction or your stock certificates in an autograph auction.

If you choose to consign your goods to auction, ask the auction firm for its consignment terms and forms. Review the information thoroughly. You may be billed for additional charges if your lots are photographed, highlighted, or don't sell. Most auctions pay consignors within thirty to sixty days after the auction closes, with an average being about 45 days. But payment could take up to eight weeks after closing, so ask the auction firm when you can expect payment.

Before agreeing to consign your material, discuss these three things with the auction firm:

1) ESTIMATES: Provide estimates on your all your consignments and go over them carefully with the auctioneer, making changes if necessary, to make sure you both agree on the value of your goods. Failure to do this could result in the auctioneer changing the estimates without your knowledge or consent. This has happened to me on several occasions. Some auctions will allow "reserves" to be placed on lots, which means that bids must begin at the reserved estimate and not below it. This can guarantee that your $500 lot won't be sold for $175; however, a reserve may also work against your lot and result in it not being sold at all.

2) LOT SELECTION: When sending consignments to an auction firm, place the material into lots as you feel it should be sold. Tell the auctioneer what you've done so he won't regroup it. Most auctioneers will lot your consignments for you, if you request it; but experience has taught me that it's best to lot, describe, and estimate the material yourself in a detailed list to the auction firm. If you consign a number of scarce items, be sure the auction firm does not lump some of them together to save catalog space. Doing so will decrease your chance of getting top dollar for them.

3) LOT DESCRIPTION: Make a brief but thorough description of each lot you submit to auction. Include historical notes or biographical information on autographs, as well as any information that adds to the value of your lot. Study the auctioneer's catalog to see how much space is allowed for lot descriptions, then use what you have wisely. Some auction catalogs run only two or three lines of information, which may hamper the potential sale; others allow ample space.

There are many auctions. Some are by mail only; others are live. Some live auctions accept bids by mail; others do not. Some auctions offer the servies of a professional bidder to bid on your behalf. If you see one or several quality items priced in three or four figures, you may want to hire a professional bidder.

Most auction firms charge anywhere from $10 to $50 for a one-year catalog subscription. The catalogs range from simple and small to large and glossy with dozens of photographs. Large or small, fancy or plain, some offer good western "nuggets"—unique, unusual, or uncommon documents, stocks, letters, and autographs. It's only a matter of finding them.

Auctions are usually fun and rewarding. I've had both good and bad experiences and have learned something new at each one.

Dealing with Dealers

A knowledgeable, committed dealer will answer any and all of your questions. Good ones want to help educate collectors and will recommend reading material, collecting organizations, and even other dealers. They can truly be a collector's best friend.

There are bad ones, too. Some dealers care little about the material they sell, don't know the field, and are strictly profit-conscious. As a collector, you'll no doubt meet a few of these "instant dealers" who suddenly appear on the market without credentials or experience; this is especially true of the autograph market. A pushy dealer is usually sales oriented and rarely has your best interests in mind; you'll be better off avoiding this type. But most dealers are good people who have committed much time, effort, and money to their profession. If you run into one who isn't willing to assist you with your questions or needs, find another who will.

One way to get to know a dealer is to review his or her catalog. The dealer's catalog reflects the quality of materials and service the dealer offers. Some catalogs are well illustrated and expensive to publish; others can be quite simple. Whether lavish or economical, avoid those that reveal disorganization or are difficult to read. Catalogs that describe an item in one line don't do justice to collectors. Those with adequate space and accurate descriptions are more likely to be worth your time. Soon you'll be able to differentiate between those dealers who are dedicated to the field of historical documents and those who are not. Never hesitate to ask a dealer questions.

As both a dealer and collector, one important piece of advice I can offer you about buying from a catalog is to call in your order rather than sending it by mail. If the item is scarce and it's priced right, other collectors will be calling to reserve it. The item may sell to the first caller. Dealers mail out hundreds of catalogs at a time, and veteran collectors know from experience that reserving items by telephone is the only way to buy.

If you have questions after looking through a dealer's catalog, ask them before you buy. Some of the things you might want to clarify include: postage and payment terms, which vary from one dealer to another; guarantees of authenticity, which range from none at all to a full guarantee; and abbreviations in the catalogs, which you'll want to understand fully.

Prices vary among dealers for a variety of reasons. A dealer with offices, employees, and retail shops in a major city probably pays more overhead. As a result, that dealer's retail prices will be higher than a dealer with low overhead, no employees, and who works out of his home with mail order catalog sales.

One concern I have with some dealers who handle a multitude of various documents is their lack of proper grading standards. A dealer who handles lots of financial documents, for instance, will use a grading system altogether different than that used by a dealer who handles other types of paper Americana. Some dealers have no grading system at all and may neglect to mention any defects on the documents they offer for sale.

On numerous occasions I have returned documents I bought after learning the dealer had failed to describe their defects. All documents show some degree of wear; collectors understand and accept this, as long as the wear is not excessive. If you purchase a document that a dealer did not describe accurately, return it immediately for a refund. Speaking of refunds and returns, some dealers and auctions consider "all sales final." Always ask what their return policy is.

Just as dealers should cooperate with collectors, so should collectors be considerate of dealers. Don't buy a document, then attempt to return it several weeks or months later for a refund. Any returns for a refund should be mailed back to the dealer immediately so the item can be resold. Also, check the catalog to see what times dealers will accept phone calls, and don't place telephone orders (or submit bids at an auction) without paying for them. As a matter of policy, most dealers will not ship an item until they've received payment for it, so collectors shouldn't expect a dealer to ship the item and bill the buyer unless they have established credit with the dealer.

My best advice to new collectors is simple and direct: Collect quality, not quantity. Buy content, not commonness. Seek knowledge, ask questions, learn. Keep a record of your purchases. Your end result will be a museum-quality collection of important western history worthy of your time and efforts.

I hope this book serves as a catalyst to get new collectors interested in Owning Western History. I've shared many of the stories and insights I've learned over the years so that they may make your journey interesting, enjoyable, and rewarding.

It's time to get started.

APPENDIX A

Types of Collectible Documents

Documents are papers that people rely upon to establish, prove, or support something. Throughout history, various types of documents have served specific legal and business needs. The documents discussed in this book relate primarily to the exploration, colonization, and development of the American West. Western paper Americana collectors focus mostly on themes that define the boundaries of their market, such as:

1) Mining

2) State/territorial government

3) Banking/finance

4) Express/transportation

5) Military

6) Ranching/farming

7) Law enforcement

8) Business

9) Railroads

10) Legal and postal

11) Personal papers/autographs

12) Indians

Some types of documents—checks, letters, and stock certificates, for example—are more popular among collectors than other types, such as receipts, deeds, and invoices. We know more about the popular documents because of collector demand for them. The documents listed here are in alphabetical order and represent the mainstream in the types of documents collectors buy and sell.

Abstracts of Title: These multipaged documents summarize all the changes in ownership of a piece of property. Early western abstracts of title are usually handwritten and tied together with ribbon and a notarized seal. Although they are not visually attractive and would be difficult to frame, their listings of dates and geographical locations might be historically important. Mining abstracts of title are popular among collectors.

Agreements: Agreements are documents that form legally binding contracts between two parties. They apply to many areas of western history. As with most legal documents, they commonly measure 8½"x14", but they may also be other sizes and may have a notarized document attached. Agreements usually bear the signatures of both parties and perhaps that of a witness as well, any of which could be important. Always examine agreements for historical content or possible autographic value. In my collection is an Elk City, Idaho, agreement to purchase a saloon for $1.00, which adds a hint of mystery to the document. Sometimes the ownership of mining claims, businesses, and land were won and lost at the spin of a roulette wheel or during a Saturday night poker game.

Appointments: These were usually issued by territorial, state, or the federal officials (governors and presidents are common) empowering another person to some position or office. Examples of appointed positions included postmaster, judge, or U.S. marshal. Appointments are formal documents, often with a border and possibly some ornate artwork, such as a government motif or a bald eagle clutching the symbols of peace and war. An appointment may also have an embossed governmental seal on it. Research can sometimes yield interesting and historically important information about either the appointing official or the appointee.

Assay Reports: These mining-related documents generally give an analysis of ores to determine their purity and content. Assay reports from some early western mining districts are very desirable, especially those dating before 1890. The assayers normally signed assay reports, and most list the source mine for the ore. Some also list the rates for gold and silver.

Bank Drafts: Also known as correspondent's drafts, bank drafts are a type of check in which one bank tells another bank to pay a third party. The two main types are "time" and "site" drafts. A time draft is payable on a certain date or within so many days after its issue, while a site draft is payable only at a specific bank. Drafts were used long before the Federal Reserve System was established to facilitate long-distance business transactions. Banks in the West often had established accounts with major banks in the East, and bank drafts allowed them to transfer funds, much as a money order does today.

Cancelled bank drafts had to be returned to the issuing bank, which kept them on file for a number of years, then destroyed them; as a result, they are generally scarce, but some have survived, a portion of them in quantity. Bank drafts can be highly ornate and may have bank note engravings printed in several colors or on colorful paper. They may also have revenue stamps on them or can sometimes have

Black Hawk, Colorado Territory, was one of the early mining camps in the Rocky Mountain region. This 1864 assay certificate shows the results of ores taken from the Calhoun Lode in the Russell Mining District.

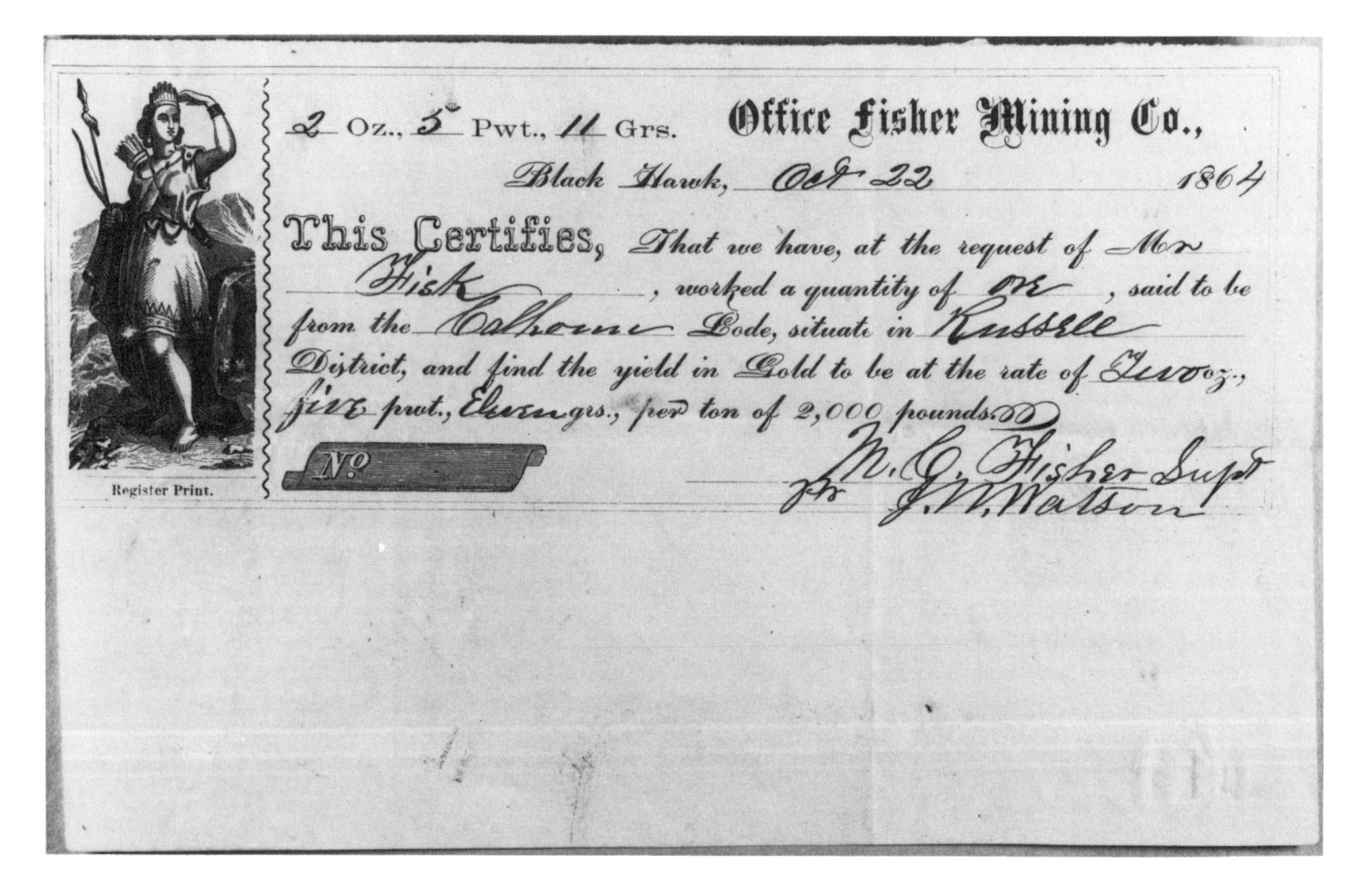

autographic value. They have a strong following among collectors, especially those with vignettes, because of their visual beauty, overall rarity, and because they are financial documents.

Bills: There are many varieties of bills. Most serve as statements for goods or services rendered. Individual types include bills of exchange, bills of goods, bills of lading, bills of sale, and handbills:

- A **bill of exchange** is an order to pay a specific sum of money to the person named on the bill. Similar to a draft, bills of exchange usually name the paying bank as well as the payee. These were originally used to exchange one form of currency for another, such as dollars for yen, or, in the days of state currency, they were used to exchange money from one state for that of another state, such as Georgia money for New York money. Exchanges range from very plain to quite attractive, with ornate artwork and illustrations. They are sometimes printed on colored paper and may have revenue stamps on them.

Exchanges were usually issued in triplicate, with the original called the First exchange. The Second exchange would be shipped by some method other than the First as a means of insuring that one or the other would safely reach its destination, upon which it would be honored and the other voided. The Third exchange was normally retained by the issuing bank. First and Second exchange drafts are more common among collectors than Third exchange drafts. You can tell which is which because the word FIRST, SECOND or THIRD is usually printed in bold letters on the body of the document.

- A **bill of goods** lists items shipped to another party for sale.

- A **bill of lading** is a form of contract issued to a shipper by an express or transportation agency. It lists the goods shipped and acknowledges receipt.

- A **bill of sale** is a statement certifying transfer of ownership from one party to another for a specified amount.

- A **handbill** is a small printed notice used for promoting a product, person (as in politics), event, or other purpose and is traditionally passed out by hand.

Billheads: These are statements of money due or paid. The upper portion of the billhead lists the name and address of the business and its types of material or services offered. Sometimes billheads display ornate artwork and illustrations. The bottom portion of a billhead lists items bought and their costs. A billhead's historical significance depends on its date (in relation to its place of origin) and the type of business that issued it. Some might have autographic value; imagine finding a billhead signed by Wyatt Earp from one of his saloons in Goldfield (Nevada), Cripple Creek (Colorado), or San Diego. I've been looking for years, but I haven't found one ... yet!

Bonds: Interest-bearing bonds are among the largest and most attractive of all western financial documents and are visually exciting as examples of bank note engraving at its finest. Collecting obsolete bonds (and stock certificates) is called "scripophily" (pronounced SCRIP-awfully)—a French word meaning to have an interest or affection for old financial documents.

A bond is like a loan to a business or a municipality. The bond certifies the loan at a fixed amount. The return on the investment comes through the redemption of coupons attached to the bond. Coupons are returned to the company at regular intervals until all the coupons have been redeemed. By then the bond holder should have received all of his money back plus interest. At least, that's how it works in principle. The financial truth is that many obsolete bonds still have many of the coupons attached, suggesting the company expired before the bond did.

There are two basic types of bonds: corporate and municipal. **Corporate bonds** are issued by private companies such as railroads, utilities, mining operations, and other businesses. **Municipal bonds** are issued by cities, counties, or states, usually for public construction projects such as bridges, roads, sewers, buildings, water works, and other improvements.

Most nineteenth-century bonds measure 15"x22" or larger. The coupons for the bonds were normally printed beneath the bond itself. In the 1890s smaller bonds measuring 10"x14" became the norm. The size was more convenient, but instead of one large document, there were three or four pages to the bond. Their coupons were printed on sheets the same size as the bonds and stapled at the top of each bond.

The total number of bonds issued by a corporation or municipality depended upon the amount of money it needs to raise. If the company wanted to raise $100,000 and issued bonds in the denomination of $1,000, then it is easy to figure out that it printed only a hundred bonds—a nice limited edition. Major projects that required millions of dollars, though, spun more complex webs and issued bonds printed in various denominations.

You can sometimes determine the scarcity or abundance of a bond by looking at its issue number and by reading all its fine print. Usually you can find a paragraph that states: "This bond is one of a series numbered from one to five hundred . . . ," or similar information. Western bonds are more scarce than western stock certificates; the latter outnumbers the former by about 15 or 20 to 1—a collecting advantage few collectors realize. Bonds are usually more visually appealing than stocks as well, and most are printed by bank note companies on quality rag paper that gives them the look and feel of currency.

Some collectors avoid bonds because the larger-size issues must be folded to fit in a display book and framing is more expensive. True, these are obstacles, but western bonds have many collecting advantages. Bonds may have autographic value. Company presidents, mayors, and other business or governmental officials signed bonds. With the proper knowledge, you can find some real bargains on uncommon bonds if you know what to look for. And few other historical documents beat the beauty of a western bond printed by a bank note company.

Railroad and municipal bonds are the most abundant of all western bonds; some are rare and others are plentiful. Mining and energy bonds are generally quite scarce. Some municipal bonds may also be rare or scarce. For example, bonds issued by the City of San Francisco are fairly common and two dozen different types exist; however, bonds from Salt Lake City or Denver are not common. Your involvement with the marketplace will soon allow you to determine what is common and what is rare.

Broadsides/Broadsheets: Announcements in the early West were often posted at gathering spots on large sheets of paper called broadsides and broadsheets; some people also call them circulars. Broadsides were printed on one side only, while broadsheets may have been printed on both sides and may also have carried an advertisement. These documents were usually disposed of after serving their purpose, and many were ruined from exposure to weather. They are very hard to find today. Even those dating from the early 1900s are seldom seen for sale.

Certificates of Deposit (CD): These check-size documents acknowledge a bank's receipt of money from a depositor and guarantee its return either upon demand or with interest on a specified date. As with many other financial documents, these are highly sought by collectors. Some CDs are rather plain in appearance while others are highly ornate. Since CDs were returned to the issuing bank upon negotiation, most were eventually destroyed by the bank.

Some early western mining camps also issued a "special deposit" certificate representing funds or assets the bank could not use for any purpose. Instead of earning interest, the depositor paid the bank a fee for holding a special deposit.

CDs may have autographic value, and it never hurts to examine signatures on any financial document. I have a certificate of deposit in my collection from Tombstone, Arizona Territory, issued to Marie Letang, who ran the mining camp's fanciest brothel. Affectionately known as "Blond Marie" by those who knew her, she sold her brothel during the height of the boom days for a fat sum and returned home to Paris, France, to live comfortably. Early western documents signed by women of any profession are difficult to find.

Checks: Most common of all bank or financial documents, checks order a bank to pay a specified sum from a personal or business account to a third party. Though common in function, there are many rarities among checks. The appearance of checks ranges from plain to very attractive and colorful.

PROPOSALS.

For building a double set of Officer's Quarters, at Fort Stanton N. M.

Office Post Quartermaster Fort Stanton, N. M. Septeber 11th 1884.

Informal bids will be received at this Office until 1 o'clock P. M. ~~Wednesday~~ *Saturday* October ~~1st~~ *4th* 1884. for furnishing the necessary labor in constructing a double set of Officer's Quarter's at this post.—

Bids for the work in whole or in part will be entertained. — A Guarantee of ten (10) per cent of the whole amount bid for will be required until completion of contract. Payments to be made monthly or upon completion of each particular part of contract. —

Plans and Drawings can be seen at Office of Chief Quartermaster at Santa Fe', N. M.— at Office Post Quartermaster, Fort Bliss, Texas, at Messrs Lockhart & Co, Las Vegas, N. M. and at this Office. —

Specifications can be obtained by addressing,

H. G. Cavenaugh.

Captain 13th Infantry.

A. A. Q. M.

This 1884 broadside from Fort Stanton, New Mexico Territory, solicited bids for the construction of officers' quarters at the fort. Fort Stanton was the center of activity during the Lincoln County War a few years earlier.

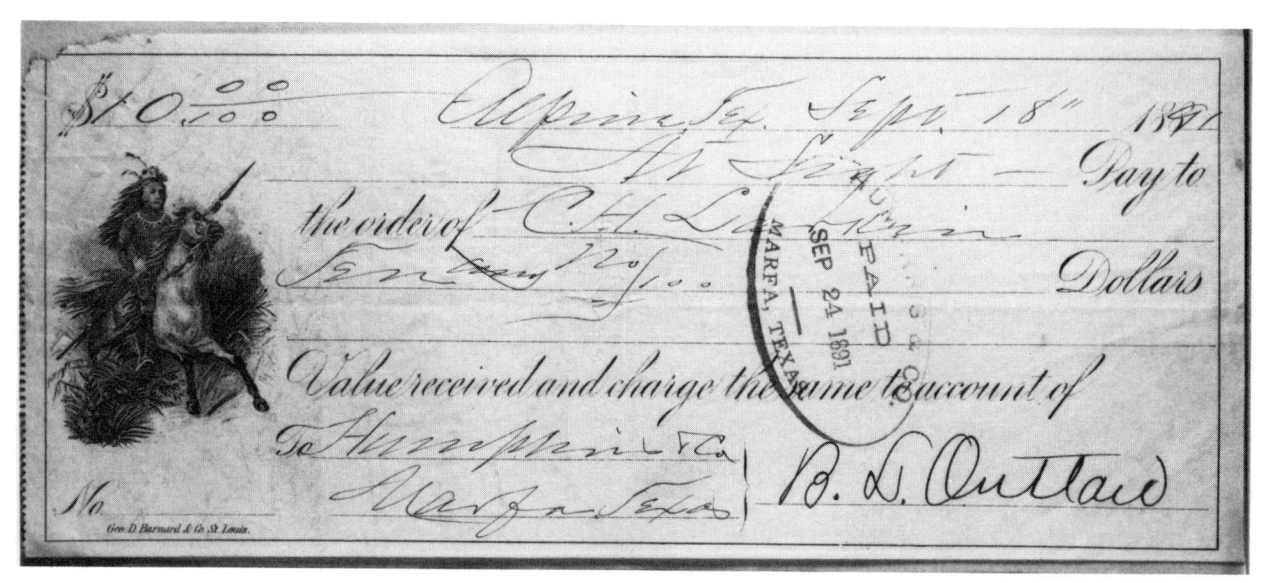

"Outlaw" seems a strange last name for a Texas Ranger turned U.S. marshal in Texas, but Bass Outlaw's disposition, especially under the influence of alcohol, gave new meaning to his name. The Rangers dismissed him for the violent behavior his drinking caused. He later bacame a marshal and got into a shoot-out in a house of prostitution, killing a Texas Ranger and wounding lawman John Selman before Selman returned fire and killed Outlaw. Selman later killed another noted gunman, John Wesley Hardin, in El Paso. Bass Outlaw was only twenty-nine years old when he died. Shown here is an 1891 site draft from Alpine, Texas, where Outlaw served as a marshal.

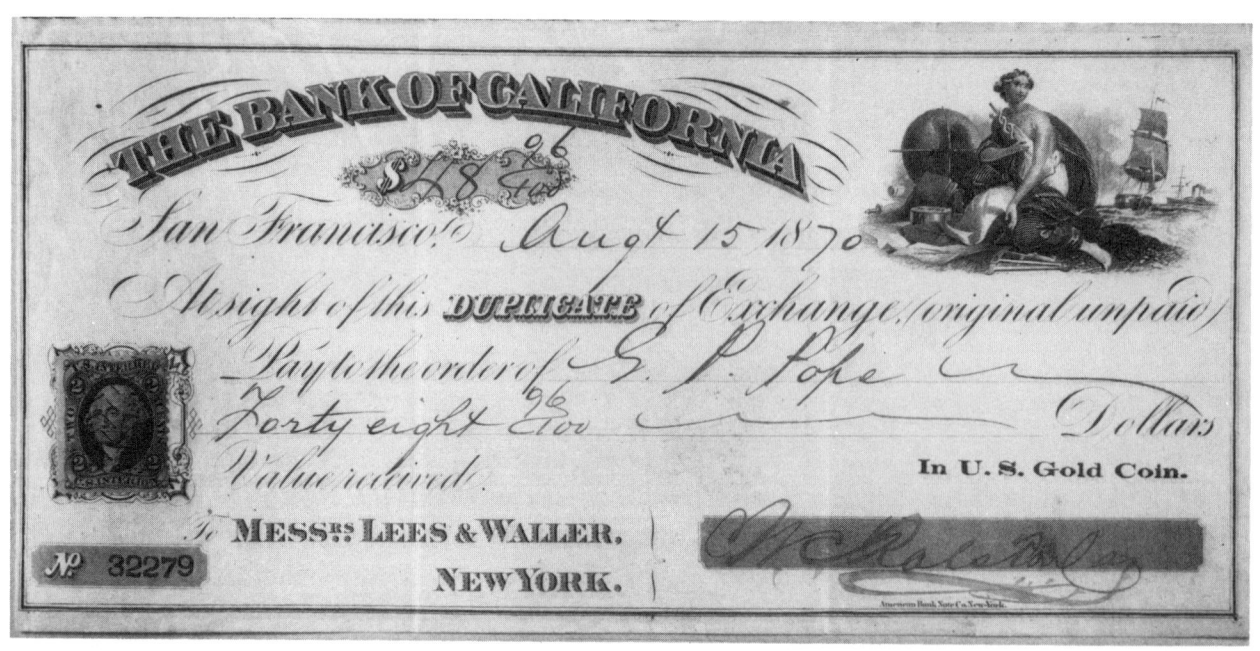

After the Bank of California opened its doors in 1864, it rapidly became the West Coast's leading financial institution and its founders, William Ralston and D. O. Mills, became California's most influential financiers. Both Ralston and Mills appeared to have the "Midas touch" and invested the bank's money in numerous projects, including mines, railroads, real estate, hotels, factories, and water companies. Ralston, who signed this 1870 site draft, became the leader of "Ralston's Ring," a close-knit circle of friends who promoted various pet projects. They locked horns with Comstock Lode silver kings James Fair and John MacKay over control of the Comstock mines. By 1876 the bank had overextended its investments and had to close its doors. Sadly, Ralston resigned and took his customary swim in San Francisco Bay. His lifeless body washed ashore the next day and the circumstances of his death remain a mystery.

Some might have revenue stamps on them, and any of them may have autographic value on either the front or back.

Until the 1890s, banks used to keep all cancelled personal and business checks. Then they began returning used checks to the customers, which accounts for the abundance of these documents on the collector's market. Because checks are abundant, use discretion as you acquire them and be alert for rarer grades and earlier dates from out-of-the-way places.

Claims: A claim is usually a two-page, legal-size document that "claims" a right to or ownership of something, usually land to be mined or settled. Although somewhat plain in appearance, this type of document may have historic value because of its date, location, content, or possible autographic value.

Commissions: A commission is a formal document authorizing a person or party to perform certain duties or tasks. A military commission recognizes the rank of someone within the military. Military commissions are very popular with collectors because they are usually signed by a U.S. president, secretary of War, or some noteworthy military official.

Complaints: Issued by law enforcement officers around the West, a complaint charges someone with a crime or offense. They were usually signed by a judge or justice of the peace but sometimes by a sheriff or deputy. Always check complaints for possible autographic value. There are many unsung heros among lawmen and judges of the Old West who issued complaints ranging from simple drunkenness to more sobering crimes. A complaint in my collection from Montana Territory accuses a man named Williams of "threatening to shoot or cut the heart out of the affiant [the person who filed the complaint] before the setting of the sun." The intended victim was "afraid of receiving great bodily harm at the hands of said Williams and believes he will attempt to carry out into execution his threats unless restrained by force."

Deeds: Usually two or more pages in length, a deed transfers ownership in land or property. Most nineteenth-century deeds were entirely handwritten, while those after 1890 may be typed or pre-printed. Typically plain in appearance, a deed still may have historical or autographic value, so always examine the signatures on deeds closely. Deeds to mining claims are popular, as are deeds to specific businesses.

While researching an Arizona Territory document signed by a prominent Prescott judge, John Howard, I learned that when his wife deserted him in the 1860s he immediately recorded a deed as if she were mining property and quit-claimed any interest in her "dips, spurs and angles."

Invoices: As itemized lists of goods shipped to a buyer or services rendered, invoices usually also state the price and terms of the sale. Most invoices are small, with the name and address of the seller printed at the top. Some of the items bought and sold many years ago sound strange to us today. One example from my collection lists gunpowder and whiskey on an invoice from Fort Benton, Montana Territory.

Land Grants: These formal documents issued by the U.S. General Land Office (GLO) acknowledge the transfer of land from the government into private ownership. Embossed with a GLO seal in orange or gold, they list the property location, number of acres, and other information. All land grants from the western states and territories bear a proxy signature of the president of the United States. Up until the mid-1830s many presidents actually signed land grants, but as the number of grants grew, secretaries began to sign them for the president. Comparing the president's signature with the secretary who signed below it often reveals a similarity in handwriting, but beware of those presidential secretaries who were very good at duplicating the president's signature; the secretaries of James Buchanan and Franklin Pierce are two that come to mind. Although their proxies strongly resemble the presidents' signatures, they are not authentic.

Letters: Letters are among the most popular of collectible western documents because of their content potential, but letters may also have autographic value if penned by someone famous. Letters can offer fascinating glimpses into the lives of those who settled the West. They describe the accomplishments, failures, struggles, and dreams of those who explored and colonized an unsettled country, as well

Fortieth Congress,
HOUSE OF REPRESENTATIVES.

Baggs Ranch near Fort Lyon C.T.
Washington D.C. 1868

My dear friend,

After a very tedious journey I arrived home on the 11th inst. and found my family all well. I was very sick, but since my arrival home I have improved some & hope it will continue. Enclosed I send you my Picture. My best regards to you & family
Your friend
C Carson

Andrew Leckler Esqr
255 Washington St.
New York City

Just a month before his death in 1868, legendary mountain man and military scout Christopher "Kit" Carson wrote this letter from "Baggs Ranch near Fort Lyon," in Colorado Territory, to a friend in New York. Carson mentions returning from a "tedious journey" to find his family well, but that he has been "very sick." Carson's wife died suddenly a few days later and her fifty-nine-year-old husband soon followed. Also shown is a signed photo of Carson.

as capturing vivid moments of hardship, adventure, and travel.

Some of the finest documents in my collection are letters. Many of them I acquired inexpensively because the seller had not taken the time to read and understand the importance of the content. Some letters can be difficult to decipher while others are easy to read. Search for those with substance.

Letterhead: A letterhead is stationary with the name and address of a person or business printed at the top. Some letterheads are popular because of the type of business they represent or because of their ornateness, which often include illustrations or fancy artwork. Collectors also watch for letterheads from certain locations. Sometimes personal letters were written on letterheads.

Letters of Credit: Banks sometimes issued letters of credit, asking that its bearer be allowed to draw a specific amount of money from another bank or agency to be charged against the account of a party named on the letter. These documents are scarce and seldom seen for sale, especially those dating before 1890.

In this 1878 letter from the mining camp of Sutro, near the Comstock Lode, an engineer wrote to Adolph Sutro in San Francisco of the recent work completed in the tunnel. The Sutro Tunnel was a $5 million engineering marvel built in the 1870s to haul ores from the Comstock mines and drain excess water from the depths. Unfortunately, by the time it was complete, most of the valuable ore in the Comstock mines had played out. Adolph Sutro sold his interest in the project and built a mansion in San Francisco, where he later served as mayor.

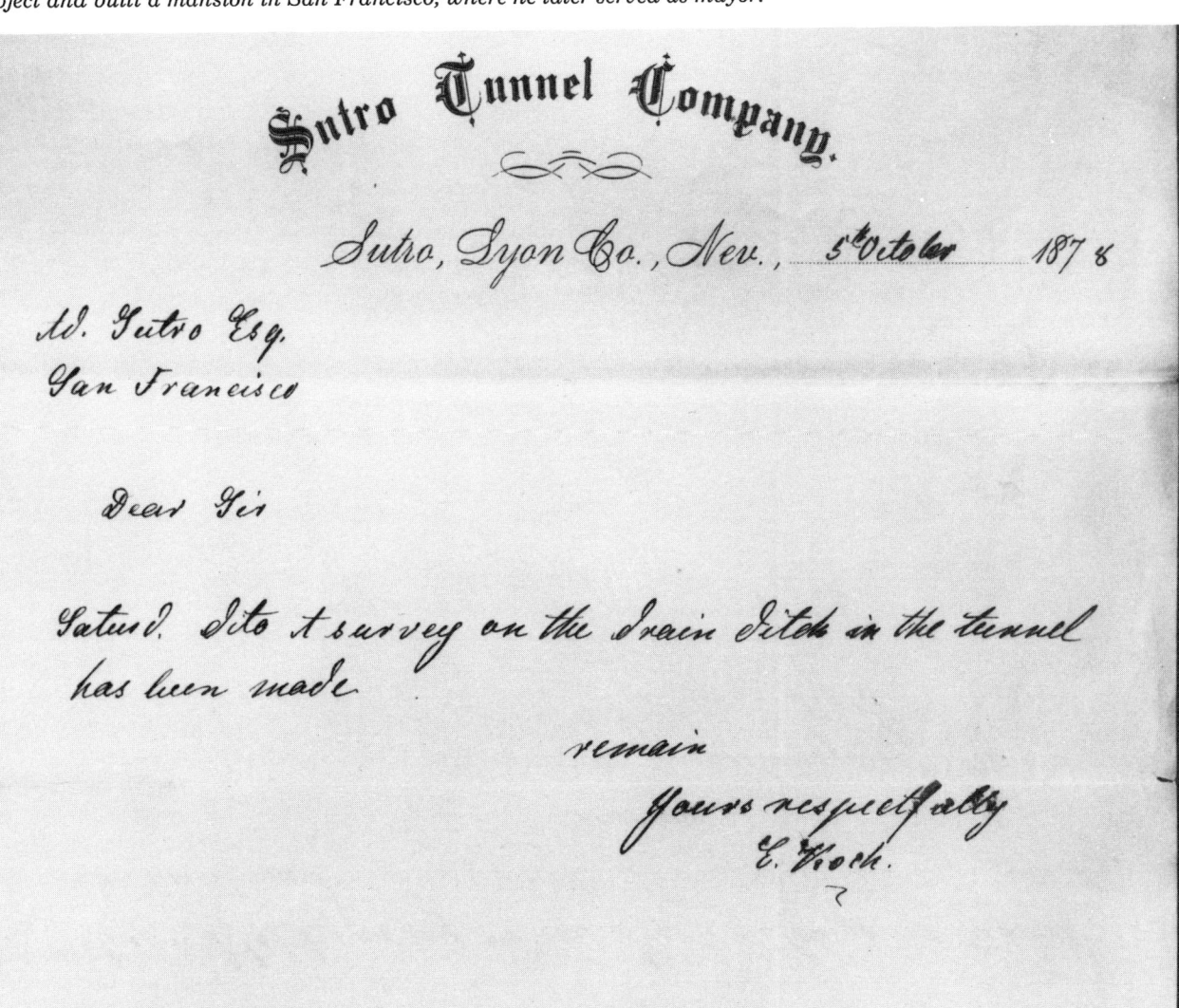

Letter Sheets: A sheet of stationery paper used for writing letters that has a large printed illustration across the top is called a letter sheet. The illustrations are usually scenes of the city where the letter originated, but some letter sheets have other illustrations as well. These illustrations typically take up the top fourth of the letter. Letter sheets were popular in the 1850s, but their popularity declined in the 1860s. Letter sheets from California or anywhere in the West are a rare find.

Licenses: These formal documents grant permission or authorization to do something, such as practice law or medicine or sell certain items or products. Licenses sometimes have fancy borders and illustrations and are usually signed by the granting official. One license in my collection grants permission to sell liquor at a saloon in Fort Shaw, Montana Territory.

Maps: The field of map collecting is very broad. Our focus here is only on collecting maps of the western U.S., which has become more popular in recent years. Maps may show various features of an area—topography, political divisions, or transportation networks, for instance—and may appear in a variety of sources, including atlases, books, magazines, and newspapers. Maps of the West may range from postcard size to wall size, depending upon their purpose.

Maps from the 1830s through 1900 represent the exploration and colonization period in the West. Though the earliest maps usually portray the western half of the country as unexplored, occasionally a few known landmarks or Indian tribal boundaries are shown. Early maps printed simply in black and white may also feature shading or toning; hand-coloring became popular in the mid-1800s. Maps made after 1860 show the evolution of state and territorial boundaries as those political forces took shape. (See the appendix on Statehood Dates and Boundaries for more information.) Many maps of this vintage were engraved on metal plates and lithographed starting in the 1870s.

Membership Certificates: These formal documents attest to a person's membership in a group, club, organization, or association. The documents are usually handsome, sometimes have illustrations and ornate borders, and often resemble stock certificates.

Memorandums: A memorandum, or memo, is usually an informal note or reminder, but it may also direct an action. A consignor of goods may send a

Coins minted by the Carson City Mint are highly prized by collectors, especially low-mintage silver dollars. The silver used in the coins came from the nearby Comstock Lode. This 1888 memorandum shows the results of ore deposited at the mint by the Mexican Mill at the Comstock.

memorandum outlining the terms of consignment and reserving the privilege of return.

Mortgages: A mortgage pledges property to a creditor as security for the payment of a debt or loan. These are usually legal-size documents two or more pages long. One 1877 mortgage in my collection offers 250 head of cattle as collateral for a ranch in central Arizona Territory. It is unique because of its date in relation to the region, which was then still dominated by Apaches.

Newspapers: Most of us are familiar with these regularly printed and distributed publications of news, advertisements, and opinions. Early newspapers from the West or the East with exciting stories or news of historical events are popular with some collectors. Most western newspapers printed between 1850 and 1900 were the same size as modern editions. Most of those predating 1870 were printed on paper made of cloth and hold up better to handling than those printed later on paper made from wood pulp.

Paper Money: This is a non-interest bearing note issued by the government or a bank in various denominations that serves as currency and is circulated as legal tender. A well-organized marketplace exists in the U.S. for collecting paper money. Because this collecting field covers such a wide area, I will mention only the major types of currency in circulation between 1850 and 1910 in the West.

Until the 1860s, **Broken bank notes** commonly circulated in the West. Issued in various denominations by private banks and sometimes by businesses or state/territorial governments, these notes were usually quite attractive and lavishly illustrated. But this currency lacked financial backing, causing many of the issuers to go broke, hence the currency's name. Sometimes these notes can be found in uncut sheets that were never issued.

In 1861 the federal government started issuing **large-size federal notes** to help pay the mounting costs of the Civil War. Known as "greenbacks" because of their color, and later as "horse blankets" because of their large size, this money remained in circulation until 1929. Nearly 150 designs and styles are known among the ten or so classifications of large-size federal notes. The classifications include legal tender notes, gold and silver certificates, national bank notes, Treasury notes, and others. Like broken bank notes, large-size federal notes display ornate and elaborate engravings that enhance their appeal to collectors.

Some western banks issued **national bank notes** with their name printed on the currency, linking them directly to the financial history of the West. Normally signed by the bank president and a cashier before they were placed into circulation, some of these notes are reputed to have been signed by outlaws Butch Cassidy and the Sundance Kid. Apparently, Cassidy's gang held up a Great Northern Express near Butte, Montana, in July 1901, and got away with nearly $80,000 in uncut, unsigned currency intended for the National Bank of Montana and the American National Bank, both of Helena. Cassidy allegedly signed "Thomas B. Hill" in the bank president's space, and Sundance signed "John R. Smith" in the cashier's space. It is possible some of this money is in the hands of collectors or dealers who don't realize their rare and historic value.

Pay Notes: A pay note, or pay order, substitutes for a check when the latter is not available. Usually handwritten on plain paper, a pay note orders a bank to pay a specified sum to someone and to charge the account of the person who wrote it. Banks discouraged their use after the 1880s because fraud became too frequent, especially in rural areas.

Payroll: A payroll lists employees to be paid, the amount due to each, number of days worked, salary, and other information. My collection includes a few valuable payrolls: one, from a Utah mine in 1880, lists a Chinese cook who was paid much less than the miners; another, from Arizona Territory, lists several Indian miners who were paid less than the other miners. Both provide an interesting glimpse of racial and wage discrimination on the western frontier.

Photographs: Western photographs can be an important source of historical documentation and are very popular with some collectors. The photographs in greatest demand are of mining operations, railroads, landscapes, cowboys, Indians, lawmen, and city scenes, while portraits of individuals or families in a studio setting are common. Collectors sometimes confuse original photographs with copies made from the same negative; originals, of course, are rarer

```
POLICE DEPARTMENT.                                    V. W. EARP,
CITY OF TOMBSTONE.                                  CHIEF OF POLICE.


                          TOMBSTONE, A. T., July 8th  1881

        City of Tombstone
    To V W Chapman                    Dr
    To Seven (7) days Work as Policeman
                                    V W Earp
                                    Chief of Police
```

The budding mining camp of Tombstone, Arizona Territory, seemed an inviting place for the five Earp brothers who gathered there in 1880 to establish themselves in business. Wyatt and Virgil took jobs in law enforcement and invited such gambler/gunmen friends as Doc Holliday, Bat Masterson, and Luke Short to join them. The Earps' efforts to align themselves with Tombstone's influential citizens only created friction among others who also had their eyes on a piece of the Tombstone pie. This notation signed by Chief of Police Virgil Earp is dated just three months before the famous shootout at the O.K. Corral in which Virgil was wounded. He survived an assassination attempt several months later, before leaving Arizona, and was later still elected as marshal in Colton, California.

and more valuable, as are original glass plates and negatives.

Various types of photographs have evolved over the years:

• A **daguerreotype** is an image made on a silver or silver-coated copper plate. "Dags" measuring 2¾"x3¼" were the first commercial photographs and flourished between about 1840 and 1855. The elaborate cases that hold them are usually worth more than the images. Outdoor and city scenes are scarce.

• An **ambrotype** produced a negative image on glass coated with a black substance. These were cheaper than daguerreotypes.

• A **collodion/albumen process** marks the beginning of paper photographs. First produced in the 1850s as "salt prints," the process was refined between the 1860s and the 1880s.

• **Tintypes**, or ferrotypes, were an improved (and cheaper) version of the ambrotype using a collodion process that produced a positive image on a thin sheet of blackened tin. These were popular between 1860 and the 1870s.

• **Carte de visite**, abbreviated CDV, were inexpensive paper photos printed on card stock measuring about 2½"x4" and were commonly used between 1860 and 1890. Some advertise the photographer's business on the back side.

While this cabinet card photo exudes an air of formality, Ben Thompson's lifestyle as the city marshal of Austin, Texas, was not. After stints as a soldier in the Civil War and later as a hired gun in Mexico, Thompson became a professional gambler and gunman who frequented cow towns of the plains and was involved in a number of shooting scrapes over the years before enforcing the law in Austin. He was gunned down in 1884 at the age of 42 over a gambling debt.

• **Cabinet cards**, a larger version of the CDV, featured a 4"x6" photograph mounted on a 4½"x7" card. Popular between 1870 and 1910, the photographer's name or studio is usually printed on the card.

Postal Collectibles: In western postal history, covers (envelopes), postmarks, and express franks are the three items most sought by collectors. A cover might be no more than a folded sheet of paper; in the mid-1800s, for instance, letters were typically folded and sealed in such a way that the piece of paper they were written on served also as the envelope. Later, small mailing envelopes became the norm. There are many types of covers, including advertising covers, patriotic covers, or covers with military, railroad or other types of markings.

A postmark on the cover that shows a piece of mail has been processed and can play an important role in the value of a cover. Certain postmarks from early western camps and communities are very scarce, while others from major western cities are more common. The earliest postmark stamps were hand-carved from wood. Rubber and metal postmarks were not used until the latter part of the 1800s. The postal service in the community where the cover was mailed from may stamp one or more postmarks on a cover by hand or machine; these include rate (cost) marks, service marks (used by ocean ships or railroads), and independent mail service marks. Another postmark is the cancellation or "killer" mark, which cancels stamps to prevent them from being used again. Certain types of cancellation marks are rare, while others are common.

An express frank is any printed, stamped, or written mark on a cover naming an independent mail carrier. Between 1850 and 1900 approximately 1,500 express companies carried mail and packages in the West. Some of these companies lasted only a few weeks; others may have operated a few years; one, Wells Fargo & Company, is still widely known today. Although most express companies printed their name on the covers they carried, only 400 different express franks (names) have been found on covers by collectors. Original covers carried by the Pony Express, which lasted only eighteen months, are occasionally available at postal history auctions for $1,000 to $5,000 or more. Other covers can be bought for as little as a few dollars.

Promissory Notes: A promissory note agrees to pay a certain sum of money to someone on demand or on a specified date. In essence, it is an IOU with a due date. Promissory notes were sometimes paid with interest or in gold coin.

Prospectus: A prospectus outlines (usually in several pages) the advantages and features of a business enterprise. It often lists company holdings and management experience, projects income and sometimes includes photographs. These are sought after by collectors, especially when related to mining, railroads, or uncommon business ventures.

Receipts: Receipts acknowledge that goods, services, or money have been received. A pay receipt acknowledges the receipt of money for goods or services rendered. Receipts come in many shapes and forms and may be either common or rare. Although usually plain in appearance, they may have autographic or historical value. Receipts of money from Wells Fargo are generally common; however, one from another western express company could be worth much more.

Stock Certificates: People who buy shares in a company receive stock certificates as evidence of their investment. As with bonds, stocks are among the most attractive collectible documents. Although

During the summers between 1856 and 1860 about 2,000 Mormon converts crossed the plains to "Zion" pulling two-wheel handcarts, which were deemed speedier and more efficient. This 1860 promissory note from Florence, Nebraska Territory, originally called "Winter Quarters," is signed by a member of the church who promised to pay church leader George Q. Cannon $6 for goods received at the last provision stop before crossing the plains.

This unique vignette shows a "miser" sitting outside of his mine "dreaming" of his fortunes. Issued from the western financial capital of San Francisco, this document conveyed twenty-five shares of Miser's Dream Silver Mining Company stock to an investor. The mine was near the present-day ghost town of Hamilton.

some are plain, most have elaborate and impressive illustrations, especially those printed between 1850 and 1910. These intricate illustrations discouraged counterfeiters and, by their beauty and portrayals of a successful industry operation, assured stockholders that they had invested wisely. Some were printed in several colors, particularly those printed by one of the major bank note companies.

Collectors may find stock certificates and bonds in three types of issuance: *unissued* certificates are fairly common; *issued and cancelled* certificates have been filled out, signed, and dated, then redeemed for payment at a later date as evidenced by cancellation marks; and *issued and uncanceled* certificates, which have the highest collection value and were usually kept too long by the shareholder, who might have tried to redeem them after ten or twenty years only to find that the issuing company had gone broke.

Collectors covet western stocks, especially those related to mining, railroads, or energy production. And stock certificates may have autographic value, since the presidents of railroads and mining companies who signed them were usually important figures. On the other side of the coin, though, just about anyone who had some money a century ago could print and peddle stocks. There were plenty of shysters selling stock, too. Another tip to keep in mind is that stocks issued from some states or territories are harder to find than others. Stocks incorporated in New Mexico or Idaho, for instance, are harder to find than those issued from California.

Summons: A summons is a legal document that orders someone to appear in court. A summons is usually signed by a judge or justice of the peace and sometimes lists a serving fee on the verso with the signature of the sheriff or deputy sheriff who served it.

Telegrams: Telegrams are written or typed messages that were transmitted by telegraph. Most western telegrams are from Western Union, which controlled the major lines in the West, but there were also smaller telegraph companies in operation. Telegrams might be valuable for their content; consider, for example, those sent by the Army during between 1860 and 1890 telling of troop and Indian movements.

Some telegrams contained secret messages, such as those from mining insiders during the mining boom at the Comstock Lode who telegraphed buy and sell instructions to the mining exchanges in San Francisco. To avoid having their instructions intercepted and misused by telegraph operators at the stations between Virginia City and San Francisco, they encoded their messages. The dramatic highs and lows in the price of stocks created both millionaires and paupers overnight.

An 1873 telegram in my collection sent to San Francisco by the Savage Mining Company in Virginia City, Nevada, reads: "Live mission do rasp invent clash exhumes fourteen,"; the recipient decoded the message and wrote this translation on the telegram: "Will do it up to last day." That's the difference between a document and a piece of his-

This 1882 Montana Territory stagecoach waybill lists several passengers' destinations and charges. Stagecoach documents from the Old West are scarce and desireable. They are seldom seen for sale.

tory. The Comstock silver kings were clever. One or perhaps several of the telegraph operators may have been on a secret payroll for the Big Four or the Ralston's Ring, both of which constantly sought inside information on the Comstock mines.

Trade Card: An early form of business card characterized by its larger size and ornate printing, most trade cards printed in the 1800s were illustrated and about twice the size of today's business cards.

Vouchers: A voucher acknowledges the expenditure or receipt of money or serves as evidence of a statement or account. Pay vouchers are the most common form; they acknowledge receipt of payments for goods or services.

Warrants: Warrants have multiple uses with multiple meanings. In financial terms, a warrant authorizes the payment of money from a company treasury; it also guarantees payment or receipt of funds. Bench or arrest warrants authorize law enforcement officers to make arrest or conduct searches. Most warrants were issued by city, county, and state governments for financial purposes. Some warrants are very attractive, with one or more illustrations and ornate printing. One that is both attractive and unique in purpose would be a real prize for a collector. I own a bounty warrant from Montana Territory issued to an Indian named Big Rock, who collected money for killing a mountain lion. Another piece in my collection, from Wyoming Territory, is an extradition warrant to have a horse thief returned to the territory for trial.

Waybills: A waybill is a list of goods and shipping instructions that usually accompanies the shipment. Railroad waybills are more common than stagecoach waybills, which are highly sought by collectors. I have a stagecoach waybill from Oregon in which the driver (another unsung hero of the West) lists two of the passengers he shuttled from one mining camp to another as a "Chinaman" and a "drunk."

APPENDIX B

Statehood Dates and Boundaries

One of the challenges in collecting western paper Americana is determining when and where a document was used and whether the place was a territory or a state at the time. Sometimes knowing one element helps you figure out the other. I own several documents from Fort Bridger, for instance; while some identify its location as Utah Territory, others say Wyoming Territory. Actually both places are correct, since Fort Bridger was in Utah Territory from September 9, 1850, until the creation of Wyoming Territory on July 25, 1868.

Territorial boundaries can be confusing if you don't know when they were created and how they changed over time. And abbreviations may further complicate the issue. For example, would a letter from "Alpine, W.T." indicate Washington Territory or Wyoming Territory? Is "I.T." Indian Territory or Idaho Territory? Modern maps won't help if the community no longer exists.

The West* underwent a series of boundary changes in the latter half of the nineteenth century. During the Civil War a number of western territories were created to protect Union interests, and, generally, the government did not grant statehood until a territory's population reached 50,000-60,000.

Here is a list of western states that includes territorial and statehood dates for each, along with other information on their boundaries. Knowing these dates can help you determine the original locations of some documents and whether the place was a territory or a state at the time.

ALASKA: Alaska was purchased by the United States from Russia in March, 1867 for $7.2 million and officially became a territory of the United States on October 18 of the same year. Nearly ninety-two years later, on January 3, 1959, Alaska became the 49th state. Its capital is Juneau.

ARIZONA: Most of Arizona became part of the United States with the signing of the Treaty of Guadalupe Hidalgo on February 2, 1848, but was not organized as part of New Mexico Territory until September 9, 1850. That portion south of the Gila River was acquired December 30, 1853, with the Gadsden Purchase. The Confederacy briefly controlled the southern route to California through New Mexico and Arizona during the Civil War, until the Union's California Column recaptured the region. As a reward, Congress created Arizona Territory on February 24, 1863, but nearly a year passed before the territorial government was established in Prescott. In 1889 Phoenix became the territorial capital and remains the state capital. Arizona became the 48th state on February 14, 1912.

CALIFORNIA: California was ceded to the United States by Mexico under the Treaty of Guadalupe Hidalgo on February 2, 1848, which officially ended the Mexican-American War. The gold rush soon followed and California remained under military rule until it became the 31st state on September 9, 1850. Technically, no territorial government was formed in California during this nineteen-month period of rapid growth. The capital is Sacramento.

COLORADO: Prompted by the gold rush in 1858-59 to the eastern flank of the Rocky Mountains near Denver, local citizens petitioned Congress to admit

---

*The West is defined here as those eighteen modern states (including Alaska, excluding Hawaii) west of the line that extends from east Texas to the eastern Dakotas.

their self-proclaimed "Jefferson Territory" as a new state on October 24, 1859. Congress refused, but sixteen months later, on February 28, 1861, it formed Colorado Territory from parts of the territories of Utah, New Mexico, Nebraska, and Kansas (which became a state only thirty days earlier) and made Denver the capital. On August 1, 1876, Colorado became the 38th state.

THE DAKOTAS: Until March 2, 1861, North and South Dakota were part of the vast Nebraska Territory. Then Congress created Dakota Territory, stretching west to the continental divide and including small portions of Canada, with its territorial capital in Yankton. In the 1880s, the territorial capital moved to Bismark. On November 2, 1889, North Dakota became the 39th state with Bismark remaining its capital, while South Dakota became the 40th state with Pierre as its capital.

IDAHO: Once a part of Oregon and Washington territories, Idaho received its own territorial status on March 4, 1863, following a gold rush to the Salmon and Clearwater rivers. The territorial capital was Lewiston for a short time before it moved to Boise. Congress greatly reduced the size of Idaho Territory in 1864 when it carved all of Montana Territory (and much of Wyoming) from its holdings and reduced it further still in 1868 when it created Wyoming Territory. Idaho's present boundary was set shortly after. On July 3, 1890, Idaho became the 43d state with Boise as its capital.

KANSAS: The Kansas-Nebraska Act created two new territories on May 30, 1854. Kansas Territory, which then included much of present-day Colorado, was a major political battleground over the slavery issue and for a while had two active constitutions. The territorial capital transferred among several communities as six governors in six years struggled to hold its citizens together. On January 29, 1861, Kansas was admitted as the 34th state with Topeka as its capital.

MONTANA: After a year as part of Idaho Territory, the sudden surge of miners destined Montana to become a separate territory, which it did on May 26, 1864. Its territorial capital started in the mining camp of Bannack, then moved to nearby Virginia City in 1865; ten years later it moved to Helena, where it has remained since. Montana became the 41st state on November 8, 1889.

NEBRASKA: Like Kansas, Nebraska Territory was created on May 30, 1854, and its original boundaries included the Dakotas, much of Montana and Wyoming, and a portion of Colorado. By the following January, the territorial government organized in Omaha. The territory lost much of its land in 1861 when Congress created Colorado and Dakota territories, but its population soared during the construction of the transcontinental railroad. Omaha served as a main terminal as well as the capital. On March 1, 1867, Nebraska became the 37th state.

NEVADA: Nevada was part of the western land Mexico ceded to the United States in the 1848 Treaty of Guadalupe Hidalgo. In 1850 most of the region became part of Utah Territory, then, on March 2, 1861, Congress created Nevada Territory, mainly to accommodate the many miners working at or near the Comstock Lode. Carson City became the capital, and on October 31, 1864, Nevada became the 36th state.

NEW MEXICO: In 1846 during the war with Mexico, American troops entered Santa Fe and proclaimed the annexation of "New" Mexico, which was formally ceded to the United States with the signing of the Treaty of Guadalupe Hidalgo in 1848. The region remained under military control until Congress established New Mexico Territory on September 9, 1850; its southwestern corner was part of the Gadsden Purchase on December 30, 1853. Six decades later, on January 6, 1912, New Mexico became the 47th state. Santa Fe has always been the capital.

OKLAHOMA: Oklahoma was part of an area set aside by the federal government in 1834 as Indian Territory for the Five Civilized Tribes—Cherokee, Choctaw, Chickasaw, Creek, and Seminole—of the Southeast. But cattle drives and railroad construction during the 1870s and 1880s put pressure on the government to open the country to white settlers. The western half of Indian Territory was ceded to the U.S. and renamed Oklahoma Territory by Congress on May 2, 1890. Both territories were unified as the 46th state on November 16, 1907.

OREGON: Oregon Territory was created on August 14, 1848, less than a decade after pioneers began following the Oregon Trail westward. The original territorial boundaries included all of Washington and

Idaho and the northwestern parts of Montana and Wyoming. The first territorial capital was Oregon City; it moved to Salem in 1852. The creation of Washington Territory in 1853 changed Oregon's northern border, and its eastern border moved west to its current location when Oregon became the 33d state, on February 14, 1859.

TEXAS: Unlike other western states, Texas did not first experience territorial status. On March 1, 1836, as the Mexican Army besieged the Alamo, Texans declared independence. Sam Houston's victory over Santa Ana on April 21 confirmed Texas as an independent republic, and the United States recognized the Republic of Texas on March 3, 1837. On December 29, 1845, nearly five months before the U.S. went to war with Mexico, Texas became the 28th state. Its capital was established at Austin on February 19, 1846.

UTAH: When Brigham Young brought the first Mormon pioneers to the Salt Lake Valley in 1847, Utah was still under Mexican rule. On February 2, 1848, Mexico ceded the land to the U.S. under the Treaty of Guadalupe Hidalgo. Thirteen months later the Mormons formed the extensive State of Deseret, which included virtually all of modern Utah and Nevada and portions of all the states they touch. The federal government did not recognize these boundaries, and when it created Utah Territory on September 9, 1850, it reduced the size by half. The first territorial capital was at Fillmore from 1851 to 1856, then it moved permanently to Salt Lake City. On January 4, 1896, Utah became the 45th state.

WASHINGTON: Washington Territory was carved from Oregon Territory on May 2, 1853, and initially included the Idaho panhandle and part of western Montana. When Oregon became a state in 1859, Washington Territory expanded to include all of modern Idaho and a tiny portion of Wyoming as well, but these (and Montana) were loped off to form Idaho Territory in 1863. Washington became the 42d state on November 11, 1889, with its capital in Olympia.

WYOMING: Wyoming probably fell under more different territorial boundaries during the 1850s and 1860s than any other western state. But the railroad, ranching, and mining eventually brought enough settlers so that Wyoming received its own territorial status on July 25, 1868. Cheyenne became the capital and remained so after Wyoming became the 44th state on July 10, 1890.

APPENDIX C

Collecting and Historical Organization

To further your interest in collecting and studying western paper Americana, you may want to join a few collecting and historical organizations where you can meet others who share your interests. Most organizations publish journals or newsletters to keep their members informed of news and changes within the field. Some associations are small and tightly focused, while others have large memberships and are broader in scope.

In addition to the organizations listed below, you may wish to join one or more county or state historical societies pertinent to the areas of your collecting interest. Information on these should be available at your local library.

AMERICAN REVENUE ASSOCIATION

The ARA is an organization for those who collect revenue stamps and revenue-stamped documents. The ARA was founded in 1947 and has about 1,500 members. Membership includes a subscription to *The American Revenuer*, published ten times a year. For more information, contact ARA, 701 S. First Ave., Suite 332, Arcadia, CA 91006.

AMERICAN SOCIETY OF CHECK COLLECTORS

The ASCC was founded in 1969 and has a current membership of over 400 collectors of old checks, drafts, warrants and other fiscal paper. It holds annual and regional meetings. Membership includes a subscription to *The Check Collector* quarterly. For more information, contact ASCC, P.O. Box 577, Garrett Park, MD 20896.

BOND AND SHARE SOCIETY

The BSS was founded in 1978 in London, England, for people interested in collecting obsolete stocks and bonds. An American chapter was established shortly thereafter, and there are over 600 members internationally. Members receive a quarterly newsletter. Meetings are held in New York City. For more information, contact BSS in care of R. M. Smythe & Company, 26 Broadway, Suite 271, New York, NY 10004.

EPHEMERA SOCIETY

The Ephemera Society was founded in 1975 in London, England. An American chapter was organized in 1980 and currently has about 900 members. Canada and Australia also have chapters. Members receive a quarterly newsletter, *Ephemera News,* the annual *Ephemera Journal*, and a membership directory, and they meet annually. For more information, contact the Ephemera Society, P.O. Box 37, Schoharie, NY 12157.

MANUSCRIPT SOCIETY

Founded in 1948, the Manuscript Society has an international membership of about 1,600 collectors of autographs and historical documents. Annual membership includes a subscription to their quarterly, *Manuscripts,* as well as a society newsletter. The Manuscript Society also holds an annual meeting and has five regional chapters. For more information, contact the Manuscript Society, 350 N. Niagara St., Burbank, CA 91505.

NATIONAL ASSOCIATION OF PAPER AND ADVERTISING COLLECTORS

Known as PAC, this collecting group was formed in 1978 for those who collect all types of paper and advertising ephemera. Annual membership includes a subscription to its monthly *Paper and Advertising Collector*. For more information, contact PAC, P.O. Box 500, Mount Joy, PA 17552.

NATIONAL OUTLAW AND LAWMAN ASSOCIATION:

NOLA was organized in 1974 for the purpose of researching, writing, and sharing interests in outlaws and lawmen of the early West. They hold annual meetings and members of the organization receive a quarterly magazine and six newsletters. For more information, write to NOLA at 1201 Holly Court, Harker Heights, TX 76543.

NEWSPAPER COLLECTORS SOCIETY OF AMERICA

The NCSA was established in 1984 for those interested in collecting old newspapers. Annual membership includes a subscription to the quarterly *Collectible Newspapers,* a membership roster, and other literature. For more information, contact NCSA, P.O. Box 19134, Lansing, MI 48901.

SOCIETY OF PAPER MONEY COLLECTORS

The SPMC was founded in 1961 for those interested in collecting paper money and currency. The society currently has 2,000 members in the United States. Membership includes a subscription to their bimonthly magazine *Paper Money*. Meetings are held in various cities throughout the year. For more information, contact SPMC, P.O. Box 2999, Leslie, MO 63056.

UNIVERSAL AUTOGRAPH COLLECTORS' CLUB

The UACC was founded in 1968 and has about 2,000 international members interested in all types of autographs. Members receive the bimonthly journal *Pen and Quill*. The UACC also sponsors several autograph shows each year. For more information, contact UACC, P.O. Box 6181, Washington, D.C. 20044.

WESTERN COVER SOCIETY

WCS caters to collectors of western postal history, including covers (envelopes), postmarks, franks, and other facets of early western mails. Annual membership includes a subscription to the quarterly *Western Express*. For more information, contact WCS, 1615 Rose St., Berkeley, CA 94703.

WESTERN HISTORY ASSOCIATION

Western historians, writers, and buffs formed the WHA in 1961 to further the study of the American West. Today it has over 1,700 members who meet annually and receive its journal, *Western Historical Quarterly*, and its quarterly newsletter. For more information, contact WHA in care of the University of New Mexico, 1080 Mesa Vista Hall, Albuquerque, NM 87131.

WESTERNERS' INTERNATIONAL

WI was founded in 1944 and currently has about 4,500 international members in over a hundred regional "corrals" or chapters, most of which meet monthly to discuss western history and lore. Membership includes the quarterly newsletter *Buckskin Bulletin*. For more information, contact WI in care of the Cowboy Hall of Fame, 1700 NE 63d, Oklahoma City, OK 73111.

WESTERN OUTLAW-LAWMAN HISTORY ASSOCIATION:

Known as WOLA, this group fosters an interest in the history of outlaws and lawmen of the Old West. Formed in 1991, WOLA has a membership of over 300 members who receive a quarterly newsletter and biannual journal. They meet annually in Denver. For more information write to WOLA at P.O. Box 853, Hamilton, MT 59840.

Glossary

Anachronism: Anything that is or seems to be out of its proper time in history. When examining documents, improper wording or other anachronisms may expose a forgery.

Anomaly: Anything abnormal or deviating from a regular arrangement or pattern. The presence of unusual characteristics or anomalies may indicate a forgery during document examination.

Browning/Brown spots: A condition which is characterized by small brown spots or brown areas on a document caused by aging and environmental conditions. Also referred to as "spotting" or "foxing."

Circular Date Stamp (CDS): A round or oval ink mark stamped on a document to indicate the date it was received or processed. A CDS sometimes identifies the name of the business using it.

Clipped Signature: The autograph of a noteworthy person that has been removed or "clipped" from the original document. Clipped signatures are usually only a few inches in height and width.

Dampstains: A condition of damage to a document characterized by moisture stains, possibly from humidity or exposure.

Docket: A brief summary or notation found on the verso of a document.

Endorsement: A signature or possibly other writing usually on the verso of a document.

Filing Hole: One or more small holes in a document made to accommodate certain filing methods.

Fold Breaks: A condition characterized by slight tears on the edge of a document where it has been folded. This is caused by folding and unfolding the paper and storing it improperly. A more serious condition would be "weak folds."

Fold Point: The intersection where vertical and horizontal folds meet on a document is a fold point. Sometimes small holes develop from paper fatigue at this point.

Folio: In collecting, a sheet of paper measuring 11"x14" or larger.

Foxing: A condition of aging on documents characterized by discoloration or deterioration.

Frank: A signature on the envelope (or cover) of mail indicating free postage for the sender, usually a person of political importance. Also referred to as a "free frank."

Holograph: A document that is entirely handwritten and signed by the same person.

Ink Burn: A weak spot or hole on a document caused by a glob or excess of acidic ink.

Leaf: A sheet of paper with a page on both sides. A folded sheet of paper with writing on both sides is sometimes referred to as a "folded-leaf letter."

Letterpress Copy: An early form of a carbon copy produced by pressing a blank sheet of onionskin paper against a damp original.

Letter Sheet: A single sheet of paper filling the dual purpose of a letter and its own envelope by being folded in a manner that allows its outside to be addressed and sent through the mail.

Lot: An item or group of items offered under a single bid in an auction.

Mounting Traces: Spots, blemishes, or hinge marks on the verso of a document as evidence that it was previously mounted, framed, or attached to something.

Octavo: Abbreviated "8vo," this paper size of about 6"x9" originated from cutting a larger sheet into eight separate sheets.

Pinholes: Small, pin-sized holes on a document caused by staples or from being pinned to a board or other documents.

Provenance: The origin and ownership history of a document that establishes its genuineness and legal ownership.

Quarto: Abbreviated "4to," this paper size of about 9"x12" originated from cutting a larger sheet into four separate sheets.

Ribbon Bound: A multipaged document tied or bound with ribbon, usually brightly colored silk, at its top. Some ribbon bindngs are affixed with an embossed seal on the front or back page. Ususally found on official or governmental papers.

Scripophily: Pronounced "scrip-awfully," this is the collecting of obsolete stock certificates and bonds.

Seal: A marking, usually embossed, which authenticates or guarantees originality or legality of a document. Early seals were made of wax, followed by paper-mounted or embossed types.

Toning: The uniform aging of paper, characterized by a light brown appearance.

Transcript: A handwritten or typed copy of an original document.

Trimming: Reducing a document's size by trimming its edges, which can leave narrow or uneven margins.

Twelvemo: Abbreviated "12mo," this paper size of about 5"x7" originated from cutting a larger sheet into twelve separate sheets.

Vellum: a strong, durable "paper" made of lambskin, calfskin, or kidskin. Generally used for important official documents.

Verso: The reverse or back side of a document.

Vignette: Pronounced "vin-yet," this is an illustration or picture. Vignettes are used especially on financial documents, but may appear on other types as well.

Watermark: A translucent design, date, or name, usually identifying the manufacturer, pressed onto paper during its fabrication. Unlike water stains, which indicate damage, watermarks are usually invisible unless the paper is held to a light.

Weak Folds: A condition characterized by severe creases and weakness, possibly even a separation of the paper fibers, along the lines where a document has been folded.

Yellowing: A condition characterized by light yellow spots or stains on a document caused by excessive exposure to light or other environmental conditions.

Bibliography

The books listed here are a small but important portion of those in my own reference library that I feel can be helpful to collectors in certain areas of historical documents and western Americana.

Barrow, W. J. *Manuscripts and Documents: Their Deterioration and Restoration.* Charlottesville, NC: University Press of Virginia, 1976.

Beitz, Les. *Treasury of Frontier Relics.* Conroe, TX: True Treasure Library, 1971.

Bennett, Stuart. *How to Buy Photographs.* Oxford, England: Phaidon Press Ltd., 1987.

Boatner, Mark M. *The Civil War Dictionary.* New York, NY: David McKay Co., 1959.

Castenholz, B. J. *Field Guide to Revenue Stamped Paper: The Western States.* Santa Monica, CA: Castenholz and Sons, 1989.

Coburn, Jesse L. *Letters of Gold.* Canton, OH: U.S. Philatelic Classics Society, Inc., 1984.

Connolly, Robert D. *Paper Collectibles.* Florence, AL: Books Americana, 1981.

Criswell, Grover C. *Confederate and Southern States Bonds.* Ft. McCoy, FL: Criswell Publications, 1979.

DeArment, Robert K. *Knights of the Green Cloth: The Saga of the Frontier Gamblers.* Norman: University of Oklahoma Press, 1982.

Frazer, Robert W. *Forts of the West.* Norman: University of Oklahoma Press, 1965.

Hamilton, Charles. *The Signatures of America.* New York: Harper & Row, 1979.

Hamilton, Charles. *Great Forgers and Famous Fakes.* New York: Crown Publishers, Inc., 1980.

Hart, Herbert M. *Tour Guide to Old Western Forts.* Boulder, CO: Pruett Publishing, 1980.

Heitman, Francis B. *Historical Register and Dictionary of the United States Army, 1789-1903.* 2 vols. Urbana: University of Illinois Press, 1965.

Hollander, Keith. *Scripophily: Collecting Bonds and Share Certificates.* London, England: Ward Lock Limited, 1982.

Horan, James D. *The Great American West.* New York: Crown Publishers, 1978.

Huxford, Sharon and Bob. *Schroeder's Antiques Price Guide.* Paducah, KY: Collector Books, 1992.

Josephson, Matthew. *The Robber Barons.* London, England: Eyre & Spottiswoode, 1962.

Ketchum, William C. *Western Memorabilia: Collectibles of the Old West.* New York, NY: Rutledge Books, 1980.

LaBarre, George H. *Collecting Stocks and Bonds.* Vols. 1-3. Hudson, NH: Privately published, 1981.

Lamar, Howard R. *The Reader's Encyclopedia of the American West.* New York: Thomas Crowell Co., 1977.

Moreland, Carl, and David Bannister. *Antique Maps.* Oxford, England: Phaidon Press Ltd., 1983.

Morrison, Richard. *Western Americana Catalogue Prices.* Austin, TX: Self-published.

Nathan, M. C. *Franks of Western Expresses.* Chicago: Collector's Club of Chicago, 1973.

Nickell, Joe. *Pen, Ink and Evidence*. Lexington: University Press of Kentucky, 1990.

Old West Antiques and Collectibles. Austin, TX: Great American Publishing Co., 1979.

The Old West. 26 vols. Chicago: Time-Life Books, 1980.

O'Neal, Bill. *Encyclopedia of Western Gunfighters*. Norman: University of Oklahoma Press, 1979.

Osborn, Albert S. *Questioned Documents*. Albany, NY: Boyd Printing Co., 1929.

Peterson, Richard H. *The Bonanza Kings*. Lincoln: University of Nebraska Press, 1971.

Rickards, Maurice. *Collecting Printed Ephemera*. New York: Abbeville Press, 1988.

Rust, Alvin E. *Mormon and Utah Coin and Currency*. Salt Lake City: Blaine Hudson Printing, 1984.

Sanders, George and Helen, and Ralph Roberts. *The Price Guide to Autographs*. Radnor, PA: Wallace-Homestead Books, 1988.

Sillitoe, Linda, and Allen Roberts. *Salamander: The Story of the Mormon Forgery Murders*. Salt Lake City: Signature Books, 1988.

Singer, Eric. *A Manual of Graphology*. New York: Crescent Books, 1987.

Specialized Catalogue of United States Stamps. New York: Scott Publishing Co., 1992.

Stone, Irving. *Men to Match My Mountains: The Opening of the Far West, 1840-1900*. Garden City, NY: Doubleday & Co., 1956.

Taylor, Priscilla S. *Manuscripts: The First Twenty Years*. Westport, CT: Greenwood Press, 1984.

Thrapp, Dan L. *Encyclopedia of Frontier Biography*. 3 vols. Glendale, CA: The Arthur H. Clark Co., 1988.

Van Wagoner, Richard, and Stephen Walker. *A Book of Mormons*. Salt Lake City: Signature Books, 1982.

Weiss, William R. *Collecting United States Covers and Postal History*. Bethlehem, PA: Self-published, 1986.

Yenne, Bill. *The Encyclopedia of North American Indian Tribes*. Greenwich, CT: Bison Books Corp., 1986.

Index

Abstract of Titles, 91
Agreements, 91
Appointments, 91
Archival suppliers, 76
Assay Reports, 92, *92, 100*
Attractiveness of documents, 10, 23
Auction Houses, dealing with, 78-79, 86-88
Autographs on documents, 23, 25-34,

Bank Drafts, *64-65*, 92, *96*
Bank Note Company printers, 16-17
　examples of *9, 17, 27, 71, 81, 85*
Bank of United States fake document, *44*
Bean, Roy (Judge), signed letter, *62*
Bidding in auctions, 87
Billheads, 93
Bills, types of, *67*, 93
Bonds, 70-73, 93
Boundaries for collections, 69-75
Broadsides/Broadsheets, 94, *95*
Bullock, Seth, signed stock, *15*
Butterfield, John, signed document, *31*

Cancellation marks on documents, 64-65,
　examples of, *15, 64-65*
Care and Conservation of collections, 75-78
Carson, Christopher "Kit," signed letter, *98*
Cassidy, Butch, signed letter, *20-21*
Certificates of Deposit, 94
Checks, *64*, 94, *96*
Claims, mining, *18*, 97
Clark, William, signed stock, *27*
Collecting and Historical Organizations, 111-112
Collecting themes for documents, 91
Commissions, 97
Complaints, 97
Condition problems with documents, 23, 57-64
Conner, Patrick Edward, signed stock, *84*

Consigning documents in auctions, 88
Content, importance of, 23, 35-42
Custer, George, signed letter, *26*

Dates on documents, 22-23, 108-110
Davis, "Diamondfield" Jack, signed stock, *55*
Dealers of documents, 89-90
Deeds, 97

Earp, Virgil, signed document, *102*
Earp, Wyatt, signed letter, *6*
Evaluation and examination of documents, 19-23

Fake and forged documents 43-51
Fargo, William & Charles, document signed, *31*
Fort Bridger, Wyoming Territory document, *64*
Fort Keogh, Montana Territory document, *8*
Fort Laramie, Idaho Territory document, *59*
Fort Sill, Indian Territory document, *74*
Fort Stanton, New Mexico Territory Broadside, *95*
Framing of documents, 77
Fremont, John C., signed letter, *34*
Fountain, Albert, signed stock, *70*

Garrett, Pat, signed letter, *30*

Hardin, John Wesley, signed document, *4*
Hickok, "Wild Bill" James, signed letter, *61*
Hofmann, Mark,
　forgeries, 48-49
　photos, *50-51*

Illustrations (vignettes) on documents, 11
Indian,
　check, *65*
　signed military voucher, *60*
Inks and Pens, use of, 19
Insurance for collections, 77-78

—117—

Invoices, 97

James, Jesse, signed letter, *24*

Land Grants, 97
Letters, 35, 42, 97
Letterheads, *37-38, 40,* 99
Letters of Credit, 99
Lettersheets, 100
Licenses, 100

McCulloch, Ben, signed document, *32*
Manufactured collectibles, 7
Maps, 100
Masterson, W.B. "Bat," signed letter, *29*
Membership certificates, *18,* 100
Memorandums, 100
Moffat, David, signed stock, *85*
Mormon Church documents, *18, 104*

Oakley, Annie,
　forgery, 44
　photo, *63*
　signed letter, *33*
Outlaw, Bass, signed check, *96*

Paper Manufacturing, 14-15
Paper money, 101
Parker, Issac "Hanging Judge," signed document, *73*
Patron, Juan, signed document, *32*
Pay Notes, 101
Payrolls, 101
Photographs, *63, 103,* 101-103
Postal History, 103

Printed reproductions of documents, 45-46
Printers of documents, 15-17
Promissory Notes, *44, 104,* 104
Prospectus, 104

Ralston, William, signed draft, *96*
Receipts, *67, 82-83,* 104
Repair of documents, 57-58
Researching documents, 54-56
Revenue stamps, 66-68,
　examples of *18, 64, 65, 66, 67, 96*
Roach, Frank, signed letter, *37*

Scarcity of historical documents, 5-9
Selling a collection, 78-79
Sitting Bull forgery, 45
Statehood Dates and Boundaries, 108-110
Stock certificates, 70-73, 104-105
Summons, 105

Telegrams, 106
Theft of historical documents, 52-54
Thompson, Ben, signed photo, *103*
Trade cards, 107
Types of documents to collect, 91-107

Vouchers, *60,* 107

Warrants, *41, 82,* 107
Waybills, *106,* 107
Where to Purchase Documents, 11-13
Wingfield, George, *55-56*

Younger, Cole, signed letter, *31*